PHYSICIANS' HANDBOOK

for Medical Management of ALCOHOL- AND DRUG-RELATED PROBLEMS

compiled and edited by

Paul Devenyi, M.D., F.R.C.P.(C)

and

Sarah J. Saunders, M.D.

ADDICTION RESEARCH FOUNDATION	ONTARIO MEDICAL ASSOCIATION

Toronto, Canada
1986

Canadian Cataloguing in Publication Data

Main entry under title:
Physicians handbook for medical management of alcohol and drug related problems

Co-published by the Ontario Medical Association. Includes index.
ISBN 0-88868-115-1

1. Alcoholism — Complications and sequelae. 2. Alcoholism — Treatment. 3. Drug abuse — Complications and sequelae. 4. Drug abuse — Treatment. I. Devenyi, Paul, 1929- II. Saunders, Sarah J., 1934- III. Addiction Research Foundation of Ontario. IV. Ontario Medical Association.

| RC564.P48 1986 | 616.86 | C86-093132-3 |

CONTENTS

PREFACE   vi

SECTION I. DEFINITIONS AND EPIDEMIOLOGY

Alcohol-Related Problems   2

Drug Abuse   2

Drug Dependence   2

Tolerance   3

Epidemiology   3

SECTION II. RECOGNITION

Early Identification of Alcohol-Related Problems   6

Diagnosis of Alcohol-Related Problems   8

Interviewing Techniques for History Taking   10

Classification of Psychoactive Drugs of Abuse   13

Guide to Psychoactive Drug Abuse History   14

Toxicology Laboratory Values and Their Interpretation   14

SECTION III. INTOXICATIONS AND OVERDOSES

Acetaminophen Overdose   18

Barbiturate Overdose   20

Ethanol Intoxication and Overdose   20

LSD Overdose   20

Methanol Poisoning   20

Methaqualone Overdose   21

Narcotic Overdose   22

Phencyclidine (PCP) Overdose   23

Salicylate Overdose   24

Tricyclic Antidepressant Overdose   25

SECTION IV. WITHDRAWAL

Alcohol Withdrawal   28

Sedative-Hypnotic Withdrawal   32

Benzodiazepine Withdrawal   35

Narcotic Withdrawal   37

Stimulant and Psychedelic Drug Withdrawal   40

Poly-Drug and Combination Drug Withdrawal   41

Chronic Pain and Drug Abuse   42

SECTION V. MEDICAL COMPLICATIONS

Medical Complications Related to Alcohol   46

Neurological Complications Related to Alcohol   46

Wernicke-Korsakoff Syndrome   46

Peripheral Neuropathy   46

Cerebral Atrophy   46

Cerebellar Degeneration   47

Pseudo-Parkinsonism   47

Subdural Hematoma   47

Gastroenterological Complications Related to Alcohol   47

Alcoholic Liver Diseases   47

Alcoholic Gastritis and Esophagitis   47

Alcoholic Pancreatitis   48

Hematological Complications Related to Alcohol   49

Anemia   49

Toxic Thrombocytopenia   49

Leukocytosis   49

Endocrine and Metabolic Complications Related to Alcohol 49

Sexual Dysfunction   49

Pseudo-Cushing Syndrome   50

Diabetes   50

Hyperuricemia   50

Alcoholic Hypoglycemia and Ketoacidosis   50

Cardiorespiratory Complications Related to Alcohol   51

Cardiomyopathy and Dysrhythmias   51

Hypertension   51

Obstructive Sleep Apnoea   51

Ischemic Heart Disease   51

Infections and Alcohol   52

    Pneumonia   52

    Bacterial Peritonitis   52

Carcinogenic Effect of Alcohol   52

Fetal Alcohol Syndrome (FAS) and Fetal Alcohol
    Effects (FAE)   52

Medical Complications of Drug Abuse   53

  Infections and Drug Abuse   53

    Viral Hepatitis   53

    AIDS   55

    Bacterial Infections   55

  Pulmonary Complications of Drug Abuse   55

  Renal Complications of Drug Abuse   55

  Glue Sniffers' Encephalopathy   56

  Drug Psychoses   56

SECTION VI. TREATMENT OF SUBSTANCE-USING BEHAVIOR

The Anti-Alcohol Drugs   58

Family Involvement   61

Program for Doctors on Chemicals   62

APPENDIX

Addiction Research Foundation Community Services

  Division Offices   66

Ontario Alcohol/Drug Assessment and Referral Centres   68

Ontario Detoxification Centres   70

INDEX   71

PREFACE

Problems associated with alcohol and drug use are common in contemporary society. In the *Report of the Addiction Research Foundation's Task Force on Treatment Services* (1978) the goals of treatment are listed as follows:

- To identify the patient

- To provide necessary emergency medical and psychosocial assessment and treatment services

- To detoxify the patient (i.e., to achieve sobriety and freedom from withdrawal symptoms for the individual) as necessary

- To carry out a comprehensive assessment of physical, mental, and social problem status

- To arrest the processes of deterioration, both those directly attributable to alcohol and drug consumption and those that constitute secondary consequences, and to effect optimal repair of damage so as to restore the individual to a reasonable state of physical, mental, and social health

- To assist the patient in developing an altered lifestyle, one that will facilitate the development and maintenance of an improved state of physical, mental, and social well-being.

While representatives of several professions, including physicians, may be involved in aiding patients in the total recovery process, certain problems must be dealt with primarily by physicians, such as detoxification, withdrawal management, and treatment of medical complications or coincidental illnesses. Restoration of physical health is normally a prerequisite for rehabilitation from alcohol and drug abuse. However, it is important to remember that treating only the withdrawal symptoms and the medical complications, without long-term rehabilitation, merely allows the patient to become well enough to return to his or her previous pattern and thus to continue the destructive cycle. It is incumbent upon the physician to ensure that, if at all possible, referral to appropriate long-term rehabilitation follows treatment of the more immediate medical problems.

This handbook is mainly concerned with acute medical issues; only brief references are made in the last section to long-term rehabilitation efforts. The handbook originates from two sources: the 1985 edition of the *Physicians' Manual* produced by the Addiction Research Foundation, which is a practical guide for residents training at its Clinical Institute, and a booklet entitled *Diagnosis and Treatment of Alcoholism for Primary Care Physicians*, jointly published in 1978 by the Addiction Research Foundation and the Ontario Medical Association.

Our intention is to provide a pragmatic, pocket-sized handbook on the recognition and early medical management of alcohol- and drug-related problems, which can be used as a source of quick reference. Our primary target groups are interns, residents, internists, family physicians, and emergency casualty officers. All medical specialties, however, have varying degrees of involvement with these problems, thus, all physicians may find the guidelines contained herein useful. It should be emphasized that this is a handbook and not a mini-textbook. It is not intended to convey in-depth knowledge on any topic; for the latter it is incumbent upon the physician to rely on his or her knowledge and experience and to consult the appropriate sources for information he or she needs.

Persons developing problems secondary to the use of alcohol and drugs are a fact of life on the medical scene. Some doctors are uncomfortable with these patients; probing into their history may prove to be a difficult chore, let alone knowing what to do once the problem has been identified. Hopefully, this handbook will make this task a little easier.

We gratefully acknowledge the contributions and cumulative experience of several of our colleagues at the Clinical Institute, which form the basis of the material presented. Special thanks to Mr. Ron Hall, Ms. Lia Hatashita, Dr. Michael Jacobs, Dr. Peter Loranger, Ms. Anne MacLennan, Mr. Donald Murray, Dr. James Rankin, and Mr. Henry Schankula of the Addiction Research Foundation and to Dr. Maris Andersons, Ms. Susan Creswell, Dr. Joseph MacMillan, Dr. Zoltan Poznan, and Dr. Jack Saunders of the Ontario Medical Association for their encouragement and their work in bringing this handbook about. We thank Ms. Donna Thomson for her editorial assistance. Last, but certainly not least, our appreciation goes to Ms. Joyce Reeves for her immense patience and skilled secretarial work, without which this handbook could not have been published.

P.D. and S.J.S.

DEFINITIONS
AND
EPIDEMIOLOGY

DEFINITIONS AND EPIDEMIOLOGY

Alcohol-Related Problems

There is no universally agreed upon dividing line between safe and hazardous drinking. Under some circumstances, relatively low levels of alcohol consumption can produce problems in a given individual. Increasing quantities of intake will, of course, increase the risk of vulnerability in terms of emotional, social, and physical damage. There has been a recent tendency to replace the somewhat stigmatized term "alcoholism" with that of "alcohol dependence." We are trying to stay away from the term alcoholism in this handbook, although we suspect that it will remain entrenched in common parlance along with such less defineable expressions as "hazardous drinking" and "problem drinking." We suggest that the reader not be unduly preoccupied with the semantic exercise of trying to reconcile the various definitions that have been proposed in the literature.

It is difficult to equate damage with quantitative consumption because there are great individual variations. Most individuals regarded as alcohol dependent drink the equivalent of more than 120 g of absolute alcohol per day. The intake of 80 g or more of absolute alcohol per day is usually defined as "hazardous"; it is generally accepted that women are vulnerable to lesser quantities (see nomogram, page 12).

Drug Abuse

Drug abuse is defined as (1) the acute or chronic intake of any substance—other than alcohol—that has no recognized medical use or (2) the acute or chronic intake of a substance that does have an accepted medical application but is used inappropriately either in terms of its medical indications or its dose. Drug abuse is not equivalent to "drug dependence"; it may or may not lead to drug dependence. While many drugs may be abused, the term is conventionally applied to psychoactive drugs.

Drug Dependence

Drug dependence, which can be psychological and/or physical, may develop as a result of chronic drug abuse.

Psychological dependence is indicated by a feeling of satisfaction and a psychic drive that requires periodic or continuous administration of the drug to produce this desired effect or to avoid discomfort. Other terms used in this context are "behavioral," "psychic," or "emotional dependence," or "habituation." Psychological dependence is an important contributing cause of persistent drug use. For any given patient the exact purpose of taking drugs is complex and difficult to identify.

Physical dependence is a physiological state of adaptation to a drug, normally following the development of tolerance, which results in a characteristic set of withdrawal symptoms (often called the "abstinence syndrome") when administration of the drug is stopped, e.g., after stopping heroin, morphine, meperidine, ethanol, or barbiturates.

Addiction is a somewhat imprecise but commonly used term and applied interchangeably with the term drug dependence. Some would confine this designation to physical dependence only, as defined above.

Tolerance

Tolerance is the phenomenon in which increasing doses of a drug are needed to accomplish the same desired effect. It is commonly observed with the intake of narcotics, alcohol, barbiturates, and benzodiazepines. Two distinct processes may be in operation in the development of tolerance: (1) an adaptive mechanism by the brain to a given substance (CNS tolerance) and (2) increased metabolic rate of a given substance (metabolic tolerance).

Epidemiology

It is estimated that in our society 90% of adults (age 18 and older) drink alcoholic beverages, 6% of whom develop alcohol-related problems. In the United States in 1976 the cost associated with alcohol use was estimated to be 44 billion dollars; the largest component of this figure was in lost productivity (55%) while direct health care costs accounted for about 28%. Of patients presently entering the health care system—hospitals or physicians' offices—20%-30% have problems with alcohol. About 10% of premature mortality in Canada is attributable to hazardous drinking; cirrhosis of the liver causes 21 of every 1000 deaths. More than 50% of fatal traffic accidents involve alcohol.

Similar estimates are not available for other psychoactive drugs. While excess mortality is associated with the acute and chronic use of some of these substances, the impact on public health is clearly dependent on the prevalence of such use in a given population.

Section
II

RECOGNITION

RECOGNITION: THE DIAGNOSIS
OF ALCOHOL- AND DRUG-RELATED PROBLEMS

EARLY IDENTIFICATION OF ALCOHOL-RELATED PROBLEMS

Alcohol dependence is frequently perceived to be a disorder associated with major social and medical problems and, indeed, for many this is so. These severe problems, however, are usually associated with the later stages of heavy alcohol use. The earlier indicators of the disorder are commonly ignored or simply not identified—an unfortunate situation, considering that alcohol-related problems are, like most other medical problems, more treatable in the earlier than in the later stages.

It is easier to identify the problem in the early stages if alcohol use is viewed on a continuum, from social drinking through the gradual development of a drinking problem and finally to the later development of severe medical disorders. For the physician, however, early identification still may prove difficult since the problems at this stage tend to be psychosocial in nature rather than the physical ones more familiar to the doctor. Late identification is fairly simple in that heavy alcohol consumption is linked with such disease entities as liver disease, peripheral neuropathy, Wernicke-Korsakoff's syndrome, etc.

For earlier identification one must look at a wide range of indices, including psychosocial, medical, and laboratory findings, from which a composite picture emerges. No single finding is diagnostic. Rather, as the number of indices suggestive of alcohol-related problems increases, particularly over the entire spectrum of potential problem areas—including the psychosocial—the more likely that problematic alcohol use will be identified.

After considerable research, based on a recent ARF study, in the field of identification by physicians the items in the following *checklists* are suggested as early indicators of alcohol-related problems.

Psychosocial Factors

- Heavy drinking; more than six drinks per day (> 80 g/day ethanol)
- Concern about drinking by self or family or both
- Intellectual impairment, especially of abstracting and adaptive abilities
- Eating lightly or skipping meals when drinking
- Drinking quickly; increased tolerance
- Accidents in which drinking is involved
- Tardiness or absence from work because of drinking (hangover)

- Most friends are heavy drinkers; most leisure activities involve drinking
- Attempts to cut down on drinking have had limited success
- Frequent use of alcohol to deal with stress, anxiety, depression
- Frequent drinking during the working day (for example, at lunch break)
- Heavy smoking

Laboratory "Markers"

- Macrocytosis (MCV of red cells > 100) in the absence of anemia. MCV is slow in returning to normal after abstinence (the lifetime of RBC is approximately four months).
- Elevated gamma-glutamyl transpeptidase (GGT) can indicate enzyme induction produced by chronic alcohol intake, even in the absence of alcoholic liver disease. Because of the long half-life of this enzyme, it takes weeks to months to become normal after abstinence. Other enzyme-inducing drugs will also elevate this enzyme.
- Serum uric acid level may be elevated while drinking.
- Elevated high-density lipoprotein (HDL) level while drinking. (Marked liver disease will abolish this response.)
- A random blood alcohol level (e.g., at a scheduled doctor's appointment) > 17 mmol/L; no apparent impairment at blood alcohol level > 30 mmol/L.

Clinical Symptoms and Signs

- Trauma (e.g., multiple healed rib fractures on x-ray)
- Scars unrelated to surgery
- Hand tremor
- Alcohol fetor by day
- Dyspepsia
- Morning nausea and vomiting
- Recurrent diarrhea
- Pancreatitis
- Hepatomegaly
- Polyuria
- Impotence

8

- Palpitations
- Hypertension
- Insomnia, nightmares

It is also suggested that a simple screening tool such as the "CAGE," when used routinely, is diagnostically accurate. Physicians can phrase the four questions to suit the occasion to elicit answers to the following:

- **C** Patient feels the need to **C**ut down on drinking
- **A** **A**nnoyed by criticism of his/her drinking
- **G** Feels **G**uilty about drinking
- **E** Drinks first thing in morning (**E**ye opener)

Even one of these responses calls for further investigation; two increase the probability of problematic alcohol use substantially.

DIAGNOSIS OF ALCOHOL-RELATED PROBLEMS

The problems associated with heavy alcohol consumption can occur in any area of the patient's life; they are not necessarily only medical and indeed may not be medical at all. If a problem is suspected, a full biopsychosocial history needs to be completed for purposes of diagnosis and treatment planning. This history should include the following information:

History of Alcoholic Beverage Consumption

- Age at which commenced drinking in some regular pattern.
- Age at which average daily consumption equalled or exceeded 80 g of ethyl alcohol (see nomogram, page 12). For women this quantity should be less.
- Age at which patient considered he or she first became acutely intoxicated with alcohol.
- Age at which acute intoxication occurred regularly, i.e., at least once/ month.
- Age at which complications of excessive drinking first occurred, i.e., social, physical, or psychological.
- Age at which "loss of control" was experienced once drinking began; memory "blackouts" and withdrawal symptoms upon discontinuation of drinking.
- Usual nature of beverage consumption, e.g., beer only, beer mainly, beer mixed with other beverages, spirits only, etc. Note any non-beverage alcohol consumption.

- Current or usual pattern of drinking, e.g., intermittent heavy (binge), continuously excessive, or other.
- Current or usual average daily intake of ethyl alcohol in grams as measured over a 7-day period (see nomogram, page 12).
- If patient is an intermittent heavy drinker, note daily intake both between and during "binges."
- When was the last intake of alcohol?

Alcohol Use and Related Problems

Consumption of > 80 g ethanol/day (6 bottles of regular beer, 9 oz of spirits, 24 oz of wine), frequent intoxication, withdrawal symptoms, memory blackouts, physical violence, morning drinking, surreptitious drinking, loss of control once drinking begins, changed tolerance to alcohol.

Accidents and Injuries

Note incidence of trauma; it is significantly higher in the heavy alcohol consumer.

Medical Problems Caused by Alcohol Abuse

See Section V.

Mental Problems

Anxiety, depression, drug overdose, suicide attempt, deteriorating intellectual functioning.

Family Status

Look for such problems as separation or divorce; sexual difficulties; psychosomatic complaints, depression, or anxiety in spouse or children; behavioral and/or school problems in children; abused wife or children. Spouse may express concern about the heavy drinker well before any other problems are identified.

Employment Status

Note such problems as deteriorating job performance, loss of sense of job responsibility, tardiness, increased absenteeism, illness on fixed days (e.g., Monday, Friday, or after pay day), frequent requests for medical certification of minor illness, drinking on the job, frequent job change, unexplained or poorly explained gaps in job history. In non-employed individuals (e.g., housewives, retired people) note any inability to perform expected daily tasks.

Social Status

Look for such social changes as loss of friends, change to drinking friends only, loss of recreational interests, change of recreational activities to include only those in which drinking is involved.

Financial Status

Note any heavy debts, collection agency problems, degenerating living conditions.

Legal Status

Look for any history of impaired driving charges/convictions (two or more are considered indicative of a significant alcohol problem) or drunkenness charges. There may also be a wide range of other legal offenses.

INTERVIEWING TECHNIQUES FOR HISTORY TAKING

Taking an accurate history may prove difficult for two major reasons. First, the patient, especially in the later stages, may make considerable use of psychological defense mechanisms, particularly minimization or complete denial of the problem. Use of these defense mechanisms must be recognized and accepted as part of the problem of alcohol dependence. Second, the physician who is uncomfortable with a patient with alcohol problems or who approaches him/her from a moralistic, negative stance is not likely to elicit any history of alcohol use, let alone an accurate one. The following techniques may be helpful for more accurate history taking:

1. Do not use the labels alcoholic, alcoholism, addict, etc. These tend to have major stigma attached to them and may stop the interview before it gets started. A term such as "problems associated with alcohol use" is more acceptable.

2. Learn to ask a few questions about alcohol use and associated problems as a standard part of any general medical history. These questions can be placed in the context of nutritional status, caffeine and nicotine use, and use of over-the-counter drugs. While the content of the answers is, of course, important, the way in which the questions are answered may be more important. The person with no problem usually answers in a very specific fashion (e.g., I have two drinks before dinner). The person beginning to experience a problem is likely to express concern about it (e.g., Usually I have two drinks before dinner but recently there have been times when I have had several after dinner, and I don't think I should). The person farther along the continuum usually responds evasively or denies the existence of any problem altogether (e.g., I have no problem controlling my drinking).

3. Learn to develop a non-judgmental approach—not always easy but rewarding when the answers to questions about alcohol consump-

tion are answered with the same ease as questions about caffeine intake. This may necessitate a careful look at one's own verbal and non-verbal language. It is not uncommon for our words to be appropriate but our tone of voice, gestures, or facial expression may express contempt, anger, or disgust. Unless both aspects of one's language are non-judgmental, it is unlikely that the patient will give an accurate history. A non-judgmental approach makes gross denial or rationalization difficult for the patient. His/her defense mechanisms may be an integral part of the disorder and a judgmental approach may serve to increase them.

4. Use direct questions. Physicians use direct questions in other areas (e.g., How many bowel movements today?). In inquiring about alcohol/drug use and problems, the questions may be vague or oblique, perhaps attesting to the physician's discomfort in discussing these matters. The more precise the questions, the more likely one is to elicit honest and clear answers (e.g., Have you been late for work or missed work in the past month? Was this related to a hangover?).

5. Be persistent but always be friendly. When a non-specific or evasive response is given to a direct question, ask the question again, and yet again, until a factual response is elicited. Provided this is done in a friendly (i.e., not angry or frustrated) but firm manner it quickly lets the patient know that only a specific response is acceptable.

6. Do not discuss rationalizations. Doing so will only divert the interview and make it unproductive. If the rationalization is short, wait until it is finished and then go back to the issue being discussed. If it is long and involved, interrupt and put the patient back on track. Maintain this strategy (again, using a friendly firmness) until the patient stops rationalizing.

7. Learn to recognize qualified answers. A great deal can be learned from exploring these. For example, if the answer is "Practically never," the next request might be "Tell me about the times when it does happen," or if the answer is "I wouldn't say so" the next question might be "Who would say so? Your wife? Your boss?".

8. It may be very helpful to obtain information from some other involved person (e.g., spouse, child, employer). A signed consent is, of course, necessary and if consent is refused the physician can, in many cases, learn much from exploring the refusal.

9. Pay careful attention to the patient who appears to be persuading the physician that there is no problem. There may indeed be a problem!

10. Answers to questions about alcohol consumption may be more easily obtained if they are included in a series of questions about other substance use (e.g., food, caffeine, tobacco, over-the-

12

counter drugs). There may be a problem if answers change suddenly from specific to non-specific (e.g., 5 cups of coffee, 20 cigarettes, *social drinker*). This person needs to be asked some direct questions about alcohol consumption.

ALCOHOLIC BEVERAGE CONVERSION NOMOGRAM

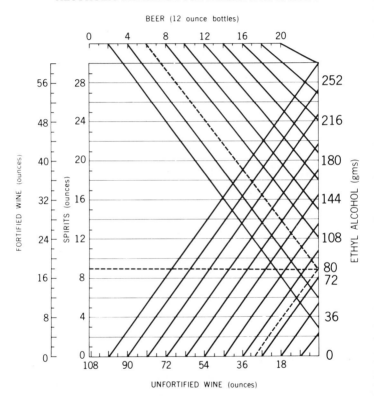

Drink Equivalent: (approximate)
4 oz wine = 1 bottle regular beer = 1.5 oz spirits

"Hazardous" alcohol consumption: > 80 g ethanol/day = 6 bottles regular beer = 9 oz spirits = 24 oz wine = 18 oz fortified wine. (It is generally accepted that the "hazardous" level should be lower for women, although it is not quantitatively defined.)

CLASSIFICATION OF PSYCHOACTIVE DRUGS OF ABUSE*

A) *CNS Depressants*
1. Barbiturate
sedative-hypnotics
Amobarbital
Barbital
Butabarbital
Butalbital
Pentobarbital
Phenobarbital
Secobarbital
Others

2. Non-barbiturate
sedative-hypnotics
Chloralhydrate
Ethchlorvynol (Placidyl)†
Glutethimide (Doriden)
Meprobamate (Miltown)
Methaqualone (Mandrax)
Methyprylon (Noludar)
Others

3. Benzodiazepines
Alprazolam (Xanax)
Chlordiazepoxide
(Librium)
Diazepam (Valium)
Flurazepam (Dalmane)
Lorazepam (Ativan)
Oxazepam (Serax)
Triazolam (Halcion)
Others

4. Narcotics
Codeine
Heroin
Hydromorphone (Dilaudid)
Meperidine (Demerol)
Methadone
Morphine
Opium
Pentazocine (Talwin)
Propoxyphene (Darvon)
Others

B) *CNS Stimulants*
1. Amphetamines

2. Miscellaneous
Cocaine
"Diet pills" (e.g., Ionamin)
Methylphenidate (Ritalin)

C) *Psychedelics*
(psychotomimetics, psychotogenics)
1. Cannabinoids
Hashish
Marijuana

2. "Hallucinogens"
Lysergic acid diethylamide
Mescaline
Phencyclidine
Psilocybin
Others, e.g., STP, DET, DMT,
MDA, etc.

D) *Hydrocarbon Solvents*
Airplane glues
Paint thinners

E) *Combination Drugs*
(Fiorinal)
(Novahistex DH)
(Percocet)
(Percodan)
Others

F) *Miscellaneous*
Tobacco
Caffeine-containing beverages,
e.g., coffee, tea, cola
Over-the-counter medications
(e.g., Anacin, Nytol)

* Note that phenothiazines, haloperidol, and tricyclic antidepressants are not included in this classification of "psychoactive drugs of abuse" because they are seldom chronically abused.

† Names of prescription drugs appearing in brackets are registered trade names.

GUIDE TO PSYCHOACTIVE DRUG ABUSE HISTORY

In the case of *each* drug the following should be noted:

- Age of first use
- Past and current use
- Mode of administration (injection, oral, inhalation)
- Frequency and estimated dose
- Development of tolerance (need to increase the dose to achieve the same effect)
- Presence or absence of withdrawal symptoms on discontinuation
- Source (street, prescription, multiple prescription, forgery, theft, etc.)
- Alleged purpose of use (to get "high," to relieve pain, anxiety, insomnia, etc.), i.e., "What does the stuff do for you?"
- What is the motivation, if any, to be drug free? "Why are you here?"
- When was the last intake?

TOXICOLOGY LABORATORY VALUES AND THEIR INTERPRETATION

The availability of a good toxicology laboratory (such as the ARF Toxicology Laboratory serving Toronto) is immensely helpful in the diagnosis and management of both acute and chronic alcohol and drug problems. One must become familiar with the facilities available in the area as well as with the interpretation of laboratory values.

Recognition of the value of serum drug concentrations for diagnosis and as guides to effective therapy should not lead to their uncritical use. Drug concentration determinations do not substitute for careful medical observation and judgment and must be interpreted in the context of all clinical data. The following factors should be considered in such interpretations:

- The effect of a given drug concentration is altered by many physiological and pathological factors.
- Tolerance develops to many drugs, e.g., barbiturates, ethanol, etc.
- "Therapeutic" and "toxic" serum concentrations are altered when other drugs with synergistic or antagonistic actions are administered.
- The "effective" range or "toxic" range of serum drug concentration may differ with the therapeutic indication, e.g., salicylates.
- The time the drug was last ingested and the drug's plasma half-life.
- The degree of plasma protein binding.
- The possibility of active drug metabolites existing.

Approximate Toxic Drug Blood Concentrations

Drug		Toxic Level (μmol/L)	Toxic Level (mmol/L)
Acetaminophen	> 4hr	> 660	
	> 12 hr	> 200	
Barbiturates			
Amobarbital		> 40	
Barbital		> 320	
Butabarbital		> 45	
Butalbital		> 45	
Pentobarbital		> 40	
Phenobarbital		> 170	
Secobarbital		> 30	
Bromide		> 6	
Ethanol			> 34 (Legal < 17.4)
Glutethimide		>45	
Meprobamate		> 450	
Methaqualone		> 20	
Methyprylon		> 160	
Salicylates			> 2.10

Diazepam
Chlordiazepoxide   }   Values reported in the literature vary greatly
Ethchlorvynol

These values, reported in the literature, may not correspond to the patient's actual clinical status because of the influence of various factors previously mentioned. Clinical "toxicity" of drugs that act on the CNS may occur at considerably higher levels than those listed above in individuals who have developed a high degree of tolerance.

The Clinical Interpretation of Blood Alcohol Level

In most "naive," i.e., non-tolerant, individuals a blood alcohol level (BAL) of approximately 34 mmol/L will be associated with clinically obvious alcohol intoxication, with its well-known signs and symptoms. In alcohol-dependent persons considerable metabolic and CNS tolerance to the behavioral effects of alcohol may develop; it is not unusual to see some patients who appear to be unimpaired with a BAL of 60 or 70 mmol/L. Coma develops in most individuals at BAL between 90 and 120 mmol/L.

There is somewhat less variability in impairment between tolerant and non-tolerant people with higher than with lower BALs. Concentrations above 120 mmol/L represent a serious risk of fatality to novices and alcoholics alike, although death has been reported with BALs as low as 90 mmol/L while some have survived 150 mmol/L.

The BAL reflects both the amount consumed and the amount eliminated. Less than 5% of alcohol is excreted in breath, sweat, and urine; most is eliminated by hepatic oxidation. The rate of elimination is approximately 10 g alcohol/hour (roughly equivalent to 1 ounce of whisky or 1 bottle of regular beer). The usual rate of decline in BAL is about 4-4.5 mmol/L/hour, which may increase to 7 mmol/L/hour in tolerant alcoholics. It is therefore possible to make approximate predictions about the time a person's BAL will become zero. Keep in mind, however, that alcohol withdrawal symptoms may appear on the descending side of the blood alcohol curve before the level reaches zero.

Alcohol Dipstick

The recently developed alcohol dipstick can be used to detect semi-quantitatively the presence of ethanol in saliva, urine, and serum. A cellulose pad impregnated with the enzyme alcohol dehydrogenase and color-developing agents will change color, from white to dark pink, depending on the concentration of alcohol in the fluid being tested. Briefly, the reagent pad is soaked in the fluid (urine or serum) and after one minute the color developed is read against a graduated color scale. Saliva is collected by a Q-tip which is subsequently rolled onto the reagent pad. This alcohol dipstick is specific for ethanol; methanol does not give a positive reading.

Although this alcohol dipstick is not yet available commercially, it should appear on the market in the foreseeable future.

Section
III

INTOXICATIONS AND
OVERDOSES

INTOXICATIONS AND OVERDOSES

"Intoxication" is defined as the intake of a quantity of a substance that exceeds the individual's tolerance and that will produce behavioral and/or physical abnormalities. There is obviously an element of relativity in this definition.

The term "overdose" implies that the person has ingested a drug quantity that is higher than the recommended normal or therapeutic dose and that also exceeds his/her tolerance. We use the term in a broader context here, one that includes poisonings with substances that do not have therapeutic uses and therefore have no "normal" dose.

This chapter is not meant to provide guidelines that are even close to comprehensive for the management of overdoses and poisonings, for which the physician must rely on other resources and his/her own training in critical care medicine. We offer only a few basic points and reminders.

ACETAMINOPHEN OVERDOSE

Acetaminophen is part of certain commercial preparations (e.g., Tylenol products and Percocet), which tend to be used by some drug abusers; therefore acetaminophen overdose is not uncommon in this population. It is one of the worst of all potential overdoses because it kills, not instantly but through a delayed hepatotoxic effect. It is, however, eminently preventable in the first few hours; therefore, understanding the way in which acetaminophen overdose works and knowing what to do is extremely important—it can save lives.

Acetaminophen is metabolized in the liver via conjugation and hydroxylation. Only 4% is excreted unchanged in the urine.

In normal therapeutic doses approximately 7% is excreted as the hydroxylation product—a step involving the production of a toxic intermediate metabolite. This metabolite is normally conjugated with glutathione. In the presence of increased serum acetaminophen levels the glutathione conjugation step is overwhelmed, allowing for increased levels of the hydroxylation metabolite. This compound binds irreversibly to hepatic cells, causing centrilobular hepatic necrosis. Patients with pre-existing liver disease and who are taking enzyme-inducing drugs (e.g., ethanol or barbiturates) may be at increased risk.

The purpose in employing an antidote is to decrease the amount of the free toxic metabolite by increasing hepatic glutathione. Glutathione itself does not penetrate hepatic cells and therefore a precursor must be used. N-acetylcysteine is now considered the drug of choice in preventing liver damage and renal failure following acetaminophen overdose (when drug treatment is indicated). It must be given within 10 hours of ingestion of acetaminophen. There is no evidence of benefit if treatment is delayed beyond 12-15 hours. In patients with nausea and vomiting N-acetylcysteine is less effective orally than intravenously because of the unreliability of absorption. If N-acetylcysteine is given orally, charcoal or cathartics should not be used as they will interfere with the absorption of the antidote itself.

Treatment

- *I.V. administration of N-acetylcysteine:* Initial dose is 150 mg/kg in 200 mL 5% dextrose (D5W) over 15 minutes followed by 50 mg/kg in 500 mL D5W given over the next 4 hours and a further 100 mg/kg in 1000 mL D5W given over the subsequent 16 hours (total dose 300 mg/kg in 20 hours).

- *Oral administration of N-acetylcysteine:* Loading dose is 150 mg/kg; maintenance dose is 70 mg/kg every 4 hours for 5 doses. The drug should be diluted in juice or a soft drink (ginger ale, if available). The most common side effect is nausea.

- The major problem in the treatment of acetaminophen intoxication is knowing whom to treat. Except for mild nausea and vomiting and some mild abdominal discomfort these patients are asymptomatic. Hepatotoxicity may be delayed in biochemical and clinical onset by up to 3-5 days. Dosage associated with toxicity is quite variable. In general, patients ingesting > 6 g should be considered at risk although typically 12-15 g need to be taken to cause serious hepatic damage. Blood levels are the best guide.

The accompanying graph plots serum acetaminophen levels against time.

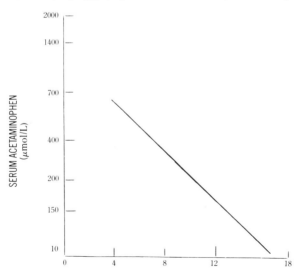

HOURS AFTER INGESTION

Above the line there is a chance of serious hepatic necrosis; the higher the blood level, the higher the risk. Below the line the risk is negligible. All patients whose serum levels are above the line (i.e., > 660 μmol/L 4 hours after ingestion; > 200 μmol/L 10-12 hours after ingestion) should be treated with N-acetylcysteine. Note that the line begins with 4 hours because serum levels earlier than this are unrealiable as absorption may still be occurring.

If more than one serum level is available, half-life can be calculated. As a general rule of thumb, half-life > 4 hours carries some risk of hepatotoxicity, while > 12 hours makes subsequent severe liver damage very probable.

BARBITURATE OVERDOSE

For toxic blood barbiturate levels see page 15.

Treatment

- "Forced" intravenous fluids $\pm$ diuretics $\pm$ alkalinization
- Hemodialysis
- Unfortunately no treatment options have been shown to be more effective than support of airway, respiration, circulation, and kidneys. Alkalinization of urine is of use only with phenobarbital and barbital.

ETHANOL INTOXICATION AND OVERDOSE

Alcohol intoxication will not require any elaboration in this handbook (see p. 15, Blood Alcohol Level). In alcoholic coma the blood level will usually be > 100 mmol/L; if it is not and the patient is unconscious, another drug, concurrent brain injury, or disease should be suspected. Ethanol is dialyzable but dialysis will seldom be required.

LSD OVERDOSE

Usually no specific drug therapy is necessary. However, in patients with psychotic behavior and where sedation is required, haloperidol 2-5 mg p.o. or i.m. is the drug of choice and appears to be more effective than diazepam 10 mg p.o. or i.v.

METHANOL POISONING

Methanol poisoning is a potential killer and those who survive may become blind. Toxicity is related to two factors: (1) oxydation of methanol by alcohol dehydrogenese to formaldehyde and to formic acid and (2) severe metabolic acidosis (mainly due to formic acid but also to lactate). The clinical problem is that patients are often asymptomatic when first seen. When central confusion and blindness occur, it may be too late for effective treatment. Early recognition and treatment is therefore very important.

The lethal dose varies from person to person; generally, ingestion of > 30 mL of absolute methanol is regarded as potentially lethal.

Treatment

- Block metabolism of methanol. This is accomplished by the administration of ethanol which preferentially saturates alcohol dehydrogenese. In most cases oral ethanol can be given (p.o. or via D-tube): an initial dose of 0.6-1 g/kg either as absolute alcohol or as a 50% solution. (This would equal 50-70 mL of absolute alcohol or 100-140 mL of 50% alcohol for a 70-kg person.) If ethanol must be given intravenously a similar loading dose (0.6 g/kg) is administered over 30 minutes, but absolute alcohol should be diluted to a 15% solution for this purpose. After initial loading, maintenance of desired blood ethanol level will usually require 0.15 g ethanol/kg/hour (approximately 10 g ethanol per hour for a 70-kg person) either i.v. or orally (equals 1 oz whisky per hour).

- Treat metabolic acidosis; i.v. bicarbonate is often required.

- Hemodialysis is urgently indicated if: blood methanol level is > 20 mmol/L, acidosis is severe (pH < 7.1), visual disturbances are present, or history suggests the ingestion of > 30 mL absolute methanol.

- Monitor arterial blood gases, blood methanol, and ethanol level q 2-4 hours. Objective is to keep blood pH normal and blood ethanol level at approximately 25 mmol/L until methanol is eliminated.

METHAQUALONE (MANDRAX, QUAALUDE) OVERDOSE

Methaqualone is a hypnosedative that is quite frequently abused. Its overdose has some unique features.

Clinical Signs

The level of consciousness may vary from alertness to coma. Symptoms of overdose include pupillary dilation, hyperreflexia, tachycardia, tonic-clonic seizure activity, muscular rigidity, and respiratory depression. Muscular hypertonicity, increased tendon reflexes, and myoclonia are signs characteristic enough to provide a diagnostic clue to methaqualone poisoning.

Treatment

Management of methaqualone poisoning follows the general principles of intensive supportive therapy. Induce vomiting or gastric lavage in the conscious patient. If the cough or gag reflex is depressed intubation should precede gastric lavage. Forced diuresis is ineffective and contraindicated. Muscular rigidity and myoclonia may be sufficiently severe to require endotracheal intubation to ensure a patent airway. When it is necessary to control severe muscular hyperactivity and this is not obtained with sedation, e.g., diazepam, then d-tubocurarine, intubation, and artificial ventilation will control the situation. In contrast to barbiturate poisoning, dangerous depression of respiration and hypotension are seldom encountered. Patients may remain unconscious for as long as 40 hours. Usually serum concentrations greater than 32 μmol/L are associated with unconsciousness but chronic users may have a higher tolerance.

NARCOTIC OVERDOSE

Narcotic abusers and addicts are prone to accidental overdoses because they often overestimate their own tolerance or are unaware of the potency of the drug they use.

Clinical Signs

- Slow respirations, from 2 to 7 per minute; may be deep compared with the shallow and more rapid respiration associated with intoxication by barbiturates and other non-narcotic depressant drugs

- Pin-point pupils

- Cyanosis, weak pulse, bradycardia

- Possible pulmonary edema

- Twitching of muscles or flaccidity

- Occasional subnormal temperature

Treatment

- Naloxone (0.4 mg i.v.) may be repeated in 2-3-minute intervals as necessary if respiratory depression recurs. Patients should be carefully monitored for signs of respiratory depression.

- Dialysis and stimulants are not indicated.

- In case of pulmonary edema, maintain oxygenation by adequate ventilatory support. Furosemide may also be given.

Many investigators have concluded that naloxone, a "pure" opioid antagonist, is the agent of choice in the treatment of respiratory depression induced by natural or synthetic narcotic substances. Patients being treated with naloxone for narcotic-induced respiratory depression must be observed carefully since naloxone has a duration of action shorter than most narcotics and relapse into respiratory depression can occur. Furthermore, naloxone can precipitate severe withdrawal symptoms in opiate-dependent persons. Although naloxone is of no use in the treatment of respiratory depression caused by non-narcotic substances, injury, or disease, its use will not result in an exacerbation of the respiratory depression (which may occur if a partial agonist were used). Indeed, its lack of activity in these cases may enable one to rule out narcotics as the poisoning agent. The administration of naloxone does not preclude the use of other supportive measures, such as maintenance of an adequate airway, oxygen, artificial ventilation, cardiac massage, and vasopressor agents.

Naloxone also produces an effective narcotic blockade. Unfortunately, its desirable pharmacological properties (i.e., lack of opioid "agonistic" activity, low toxicity) are outweighed by its short duration of action, necessitating high doses and/or frequent repeated administration.

Dosage of naloxone (for emergency situations) is 0.4 mg (1 mL) i.v. This may be repeated in 2 to 3 minutes if the desired degree of counteraction and improvement in respiratory function is not obtained immediately. Failure to obtain significant improvement after 2 to 3 doses suggests that the condition may be due partly or completely to other diseases, processes, or non-narcotic drugs. Since the duration of action of narcotics may exceed that of naloxone, the patient should be kept under continual surveillance and repeated doses of naloxone should be administered as necessary.

RELATIVE *ANALGESIC* POTENCIES OF NARCOTICS
(equivalent to 10 mg morphine i.m.)

Generic Name	Brand Name	i.m.(mg)	p.o.(mg)
Alphaprodine	Nisentil	45	N/A
Codeine	—	130	200
Heroin	—	3	18
Hydromorphone	Dilaudid	1.5	7.5
Levorphanol	Levo-Dromoran	2	4
Meperidine	Demerol	75	200
Methadone	—	N/A	20
Morphine	—	10	30
Oxycodone (+ other ingredients)	Percodan	N/A	30
Pentazocine	Talwin	60	180

PHENCYCLIDINE (PCP) OVERDOSE

Phencyclidine has been appearing increasingly on the street scene, and for this reason a review of this hallucinogen is given. Phencyclidine was developed as an animal anaesthetic and made available under the brand name of Sernyl by Parke, Davis & Co. It first appeared on the street drug scene in 1967 as a hallucinogen, synthesized primarily in illicit laboratories. Mis-synthesis yields a product that causes abdominal cramps, emesis (frequently containing blood), coma, and death.

Phencyclidine—also known as the peace pill, PCP, hog, and angel dust—may be smoked, taken orally, i.m., or i.v. It is found as a contaminant and is falsely represented as mescaline, LSD, psilocybin, and tetrahydrocannabinol. PCP is a white stable solid, readily soluble in water, alcohol, and chloroform. It is slowly metabolized, having a half-life of 18 to 19 hours. The dosage, route of administration, and time ingested play significant roles in its effect on the patient. With low doses, it produces a state resembling alcohol intoxication, including muscular inco-ordination and generalized numbness of the extremities. With larger doses, analgesia and anaesthesia with sensory disturbances occurs as well as muscular rigidity. A loss of contact with the environment and a feeling of isolation ensue. The patient is confused, may hallucinate, may stare into space or be agitated, may be grimacing—generally resembling an acute schizophrenic. There may be intermittent acute increases in muscle tone, extensor spasm, and ankle clonus. Excessive bronchial secretions coupled with muscle spasm may produce cyanosis and respiratory difficulties. With very large doses coma may occur.

The diagnosis of PCP poisoning should be considered in any drug-abusing patient with some of the above symptomatology and, indeed, with any kind of bizarre behavior.

Recovery is slow because of the long half-life of PCP. Treatment is largely that of supportive observation. Respiratory status must be closely watched; excessive bronchial secretions may have to be suctioned. If possible it is best to leave the patient alone in a quiet room to minimize stimuli. In cases of severe agitation the administration of haloperidol or diazepam may be necessary.

SALICYLATE OVERDOSE

Overdose with salicylates alone is not common among chronic drug abusers, but it may occur as part of an overdose with a combination drug preparation. Keep the patient under observation if salicylate level is > 2 mmol/L within 6 hours, if dose taken is > 150 mg/kg, and if methyl salicylate was taken (oil of Wintergreen). If serum salicylate level is > 2 mmol/L, repeat the test after 2 hours.

Blood levels: 3-4.5 mmol/L = mild intoxication, 4.5-7 mmol/L = moderate intoxication, and > 7 mmol/L = severe intoxication.

Treatment

- Usually supportive therapy is sufficient for salicylate concentration < 4 mmol/L. The rate of salicylate metabolism becomes progressively slower if the blood concentration is higher; half-life of elimination increases from 4 to 16 hours. Therefore, hemodialysis should be considered immediately in patients with concentrations > 7 mmol/L.

- "Forced" intravenous fluids ± diuretics ± alkalinization of urine.

- Important that the patient not become acidotic since acidosis causes increased amounts of salicylate to enter cells.

- The following blood work should be done immediately and q 2 hours in severe salicylate overdose: electrolytes, blood sugar, salicylate concentration, blood gases, and prothrombin time.

- Aqua mephyton 10 mg s.c. should be given.

- Continue treatment until the salicylate level is less than 2 mmol/L.

TRICYCLIC ANTIDEPRESSANT OVERDOSE

Tricyclic antidepressants include imipramine, nortriptyline, doxepin, and amitriptyline. Special clinical problems are coma, cardiac arrhythmias, and anticholinergic effects.

These patients should be placed on a cardiac monitor for at least 24 hours post-ingestion. Both tachy- and brady-arrhythmias may occur. Some of the manifestations of cardiotoxicity associated with electrocardiographic changes include flattening or inversion of the T wave, bundle branch block, heart blocks, ventricular tachycardia, and ventricular fibrillation. Myocardial infarction, orthostatic hypotension, and stroke have also been reported. Treatment of arrhythmias in tricyclic overdose is identical with treatment of the same arrhythmias occurring under other circumstances. Patients should not be discharged in less than 3 days.

In severe tricyclic poisoning, particularly in comatose patients, the administration of the anti-cholinesterase drug physostigmine (2 mg i.m. or slow i.v. injection) has been reported to reverse the severe anticholinergic CNS effects of the tricyclics and wake up the patient. Unfortunately the effect of physostigmine lasts only a short time, and frequent (e.g., q 30-60 minutes) doses are required for maintenance. It is debatable whether it ultimately alters the outcome in most cases.

Section
IV

WITHDRAWAL

WITHDRAWAL

Once the existence of an alcohol or drug problem has been recognized, the next step in the recovery process is the detoxification of the patient, i.e., the withdrawal of the substance(s) in question. Whether or not this is accomplished abruptly, by gradual tapering, or by some temporary pharmacological substitute will depend on the substance and also on the patient's clinical circumstances. As for the former, the physician must know some elementary pharmacological principles and, with regard to the latter, a great deal of clinical judgment will be required. The goal is always to accomplish the detoxification process in a way that is safe for the patient as well as humane, in order to minimize his or her discomfort. Although we are frequently disappointed, detoxification should be undertaken with the optimistic assumption that it is the beginning of a successful recovery.

In this section we offer some guidelines on this all-important phase of treatment—withdrawal from alcohol and other abused psychoactive drugs.

ALCOHOL WITHDRAWAL

The severity of alcohol withdrawal varies from patient to patient and even from one occasion to another for the same patient; the duration and intensity of preceding alcohol exposure is one determining factor. Mild reactions—usually lasting up to 48 hours—consist of insomnia, irritability, and tremor. In severe withdrawal, however, these symptoms may be followed by auditory, visual, or tactile hallucinations, seizures (see page 30), and global confusion (delirium). Stress responses (increased catecholmine discharge, hyperadrenergic phenomena, e.g., tachycardia, perspiration, increased blood pressure) often accompany withdrawal reactions.

Outpatient and Emergency Management

Many patients with mild withdrawal can be managed safely and effectively at home or in non-medical detoxification centres (see listing in Appendix). In such cases thiamine (50 mg) and diazepam (20 mg p.o.) may be given, and the patient should be observed for 2 hours and then sent home/detoxification centre with a prescription for 2 or 3 additional doses of diazepam (q 1-2 hours prn). If possible, a relative or friend should be enlisted to watch the patient during the withdrawal phase. If the response is not adequate at the end of 2 hours, the patient ideally should be admitted to hospital.

Indications for Hospitalization for Alcohol Withdrawal

- Presence of associated medical or surgical conditions requiring treatment
- Hallucinations, tachycardia (> 110 per minute), severe tremor, extreme agitation, history of severe withdrawal symptoms
- Fever > 38.0°C

- Ataxia, nystagmus, confusion, and ophthalmoplegia (Wernicke's encephalopathy)
- Confusion or delirium
- Seizures: generalized seizure occurring for the first time in the withdrawal state, focal seizures, status epilepticus, seizures in patients withdrawing from a combination of alcohol and other drugs
- Recent history of head injury with loss of consciousness
- Physical dependence on other drugs
- Occasional "social" indication, e.g., it is thought to be unlikely that the patient will be capable of discontinuing drinking on his or her own.

Withdrawal Syndrome—Hospital Treatment

Assessment

Look for infection, trauma, pancreatitis, dehydration, electrolyte abnormalities, hypoglycemia, hyperthermia, aspiration, and arrhythmias.

General Treatment

- Reassurance, supportive nursing care
- Dimly lit, quiet, single room, if possible
- Vital signs; cardiac monitor if arrhythmias are present
- Thiamine (50 mg) parenterally or p.o.
- Hydration may be required, although in milder withdrawal overhydration is more typical
- Correct electrolytes; replacement of potassium is indicated in hypokalemic patients with symptoms of cardiac arrhythmias and in those receiving digitalis

Pharmacotherapy for Withdrawal Symptoms

While supportive nursing care alone is often effective, many patients will require some pharmacotherapy. For moderate to severe withdrawal we prefer the multiple oral "loading" technique using diazepam, 20 mg q 1-2 hours to a minimum cumulative dose of 60 mg or until reasonable symptomatic relief is obtained. The rationale behind this approach is that relatively large doses of the drug are administered when it is most needed; the long half-life of diazepam (average, approximately 40 hours) will allow gradual pharmacokinetic self-tapering without the need for additional doses. The effectiveness of diazepam (and the end-point of loading) can be judged clinically.

In case of extreme agitation or inability to take it orally, diazepam can be given i.v. slowly (5 mg/min) until the patient is calm; subsequent doses must be individualized on the basis of the clinical picture.

If dosages are not adjusted carefully, excessive drowsiness, lethargy, ataxia, diplopia, and confusion may occur. Respiratory depression and increased risk of aspiration are hazards to be avoided. Excessive central nervous system depression is usually preventable by individual adjustment of dosage to the clinical state of the patient.

Lower dosages might be required in patients with severe liver disease and a low serum albumin since the concentration of free active diazepam may be higher and it is metabolized more slowly in patients with cirrhosis. For these patients the use of a benzodiazepine whose metabolism is not altered by liver disease and with a short half-life might be considered (e.g., oxazepam 15-30 mg t.i.d. or lorazepam 1-2 mg t.i.d.).

The phenothiazines and butyrophenones seem to have antihallucinatory activity in alcohol withdrawal and alcoholic hallucinosis. However, they lower the seizure threshold. Butyrophenones (haloperidol) cause less sedation and hypotension than chlorpromazine and therefore can be reasonably tried for the control of hallucinations, particularly after the risk of seizures has passed (i.e., after 3 days). Diazepam may be given with haloperidol to treat other symptoms of withdrawal and thus prevent or decrease potential seizure activity. The dose of haloperidol is 2-5 mg (i.m. or p.o.) q 1-2 hours prn (maximum of 5 doses).

Alcohol Withdrawal Seizures

Seizures during alcohol withdrawal reactions are typically grand mal, non-focal, and one or two in number and occur between 12 and 60 hours after cessation of drinking. They require treatment if they are repeated, continuous, or life-threatening. There is uncertainty about the therapeutic and prophylactic value of phenytoin in alcohol withdrawal seizures.

In most patients *without a previous history of seizures*, benzodiazepines alone as used for alcohol withdrawal probably have sufficient anticonvulsant activity to prevent withdrawal seizures.

In patients *with a previous history of withdrawal seizures*, the prophylactic use of phenytoin (in addition to benzodiazepines) has been an accepted practice; after a loading dose of 10 mg/kg, 300 mg of phenytoin p.o. for 5 days has been judged to be sufficient and effective for this purpose. Our current practice, however, is not to use prophylactic phenytoin in patients with a history of withdrawal seizures; instead, we administer 3 x 20 mg oral loading of diazepam at hourly intervals for seizure prophylaxis, regardless of the severity of withdrawal symptoms. (Further diazepam administration will, of course, be dependent on the severity of withdrawal, as indicated earlier.) The same applies to patients presenting shortly after a withdrawal seizure.

The patient who *seizures for the first time* in his/her life—even if it is likely a withdrawal seizure—should have a "seizure work-up" to rule out organic disease and a structural lesion; keep in mind that an alcoholic too can have a brain tumor. The work-up should consist of routine hematology, blood sugar, BUN, electrolytes, serum Ca, Mg, skull x-rays, EEG, and CT scan as well as drug screening.

If there is a history of idiopathic epilepsy, the patient should continue with his/her regular anticonvulsant medication(s).

The patient who has *multiple (i.e., more than 2) seizures* during one admission should be given phenytoin treatment; load with 10 mg/kg, half of which can be given orally, the other half i.v., e.g., for a 60-kg man 300 mg i.v., 300 mg p.o., and continue with 300 mg phenytoin p.o. per day for 5 days. In the meantime do a seizure work-up as outlined above. Whether or not to continue with phenytoin will depend on the eventual diagnosis; if it is "alcohol withdrawal seizure," phenytoin should not be continued.

For *status epilepticus* give diazepam 10 mg i.v. slowly (5 mg/min), watching for respiratory depression and also load with phenytoin. Severe status epilepticus needs intubation, general anaesthesia, and curarization; such patients should be transferred to an intensive care unit.

Patients with *focal seizures* should be admitted and given a full work-up unless previously conducted for the same kind of focal seizures.

Those patients who are withdrawing from *alcohol and other drugs* (particularly hypnosedatives and benzodiazepines) should be admitted because withdrawal seizures from more than one substance can be more serious and difficult to manage. Withdrawal management of these other substances will be discussed below. N.B.: Phenothiazines, butyrophenones, and phenytoin are ineffective in hypnosedative and benzodiazepine withdrawal and should be avoided.

Summary Chart

The simple diagram below summarizes our recommended basic approach to
the pharmacotherapy of alcohol withdrawal.

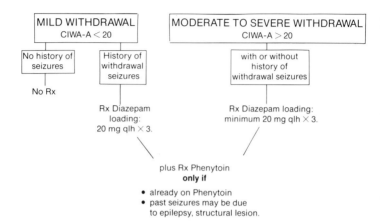

CIWA-A

CIWA-A (Clinical Withdrawal Assessment for Alcohol), originally developed
as a research tool, is a 15-item rating scale for the assessment of the severity
of withdrawal and is available on request. Many physicians can distinguish
reasonably well between mild and moderate to severe withdrawal on the basis
of clinical judgment alone, without the use of a scoring system.

SEDATIVE-HYPNOTIC WITHDRAWAL

Sedative-hypnotics are broadly divided into barbiturates and non-barbitu-
rates (see classification on page 13); individuals thought to be dependent on
either group of drugs are treated identically in terms of withdrawal management. Chronic use of these drugs results in considerable tolerance; if the
tolerance level for an individual is exceeded, intoxication results.

Clinical Manifestations of Acute and Chronic Hypnotic Intoxication

- Lethargy
- Hypotonia, dysmetria, and decreased superficial reflexes
- Vertigo
- Ataxic gait with positive Rhomberg sign
- Nystagmus, diplopia, strabismus

- Slurred speech
- Impaired judgment
- Emotional lability

Sensation, deep tendon reflexes, and pupillary reflexes are usually unaltered. The symptoms resemble those of alcohol intoxication.

If a chronically dependent individual stops taking the drug abruptly, there is a risk of severe and life-threatening withdrawal syndrome.

Symptoms and Signs of Sedative-Hypnotic Withdrawal

Minor	**Major**
(Onset typically 1-3 days after discontinuing hypnosedatives)	(Onset usually 2 or 3 days after discontinuing hypnosedatives; seldom occurs without preceding minor withdrawal symptoms)
• Anxiety	
• Hyperreflexia	• Any or all of the signs or symptoms of minor withdrawal, plus
• Insomnia	
• Muscle twitches	• Tonic-clonic seizure(s) and/or delirium characterized by agitation, delusions, disorientation, hallucinations, and hyperpyrexia; may cause death from cardiovascular collapse
• Restlessness	
• Tremor	
• Diaphoresis	
• Slight elevation of temperature	
• Anorexia	
• Nausea	
• Vomiting	

Withdrawal seizures usually occur on the 2nd or 3rd day of withdrawal but may occur earlier or may be delayed to the 7th or 8th day. Unexplained seizures in adults should always prompt the physician to consider withdrawal from chronic sedative-hypnotic drug abuse. Urine and blood for drug screening will aid in making the diagnosis in patients who cannot or do not give a reliable history. Phenothiazines, butyrophenones, and phenytoin are ineffective for the management of hypnotic withdrawal seizures and should be avoided. However, phenytoin should be used if there is a history of seizure disorder unrelated to drug abuse. Some patients who have seizures (50%) develop delirium and hyperpyrexia (4th-7th day of withdrawal) if not treated. The incidence of seizures, delirium, and hyperpyrexia increases after continuous intoxication with large doses of sedative-hypnotics.

Acute hypnotic (barbiturate and non-barbiturate) poisoning may be superimposed on chronic intoxication in the dependent person. These patients should be observed in the recovery phase for withdrawal. For patients with combined sedative-hypnotic and narcotic dependence, withdraw one drug at a time (for example, maintain the patient on the narcotic while withdrawing from barbiturates).

There are no reliable quantitative criteria by which one can predict which patient is at risk of developing a severe withdrawal reaction. As a general guide, one should count on this risk in any patient who has taken the equivalent of 500 mg/day of a short- or intermediate-acting barbiturate (e.g., secobarbital) for at least a month. But then the histories are seldom clearcut or reliable; gross over- as well as understatement of dosages may be given. Abrupt withdrawal in a chronically dependent individual is dangerous and contraindicated; the decision, however, about who is or who is not chronically dependent and therefore at risk for severe withdrawal is often arbitrary and based on clinical judgment and sometimes on guesswork. Since our current suggested treatment method of *phenobarbital-loading* (see page 35) entails very little danger of overdosing, we recommend that the physician, if in doubt, err on the side of treating unnecessarily. The purpose of phenobarbital loading is to mildly intoxicate the patient to *prevent* major withdrawal reactions *before* they occur. The criteria below can be used as a general guide.

Criteria for Phenobarbital Loading

Major Criteria

- Seizures
- Delirium
- History of seizures or delirium when withdrawing from the same type of drug

Minor Criteria

- Barbiturate dose > 500 mg/day
- Duration > 1 month
- Concurrent abuse of other hypnosedatives
- Clinical tolerance with "toxic" drug levels
- Evidence of withdrawal: anxiety, restlessness, insomnia, nausea and vomiting, tremor, diaphoresis, confusion, hallucination, hyperreflexia

Advantages of Phenobarbital Loading

- Effective
- Safe
- Simple and objective
- No reinforcement of drug-taking behavior

- Shorter period of medical supervision

- Slow rate of elimination of phenobarbital (average half-life 86 hours)
  minimizes fluctuation in clinical status
  can be used to reassure patient (and physician)

- Loading dose of phenobarbital indicates the degree of physical dependence

- Phenobarbital has
  low abuse potential
  wide margin of safety
  superior anticonvulsant properties

Instructions for Phenobarbital Loading

Drug screen should be done, if possible, before phenobarbital loading. The blood level of the drug(s) of abuse should be correlated with the patient's clinical status.

Begin loading when barbiturate level is below "toxic" value.

Oral Loading
120 mg phenobarbital orally every hour (1.8 mg/kg) in a patient of normal weight (70 kg). In excessively obese or underweight patients increase this dose to approximately 2.4 mg/kg/hour to ensure efficient loading. Clinically assess the patient every hour or prior to each oral dose. Discontinue phenobarbital when patient exhibits three or more of the following signs: asleep but arousable, nystagmus, dysarthria, ataxia, drowsiness, or emotional lability. In our experience, no supplementary doses of phenobarbital will be needed once this end-point has been reached.

Continuous I.V. Method
2.4 mg/kg/hour (concentration 10 mg/mL N saline) to obtain same end-point as with oral administration. If patient is in major withdrawal initially give phenobarbital 1.75 mg/kg i.v. push over 5 minutes and then the continuous infusion. The intravenous method is used if oral administration is impossible, contraindicated, or if the situation is medically urgent, e.g., seizures, delirium.

BENZODIAZEPINE WITHDRAWAL

Benzodiazepines are very commonly prescribed drugs for anxiolytic and hypnotic purposes. Their abuse potential has been increasingly recognized in recent years; there are many individuals who develop strong psychological dependence on these drugs. Tolerance, with need to increase the dose, evolves in many cases; it is not uncommon to see patients who regularly ingest far more than 100 mg of diazepam or an equivalent dose of another benzodiazepine per day.

The question of physical dependence on benzodiazepines is somewhat uncertain. Chronic abusers, who abruptly discontinue these drugs, in many cases show severe anxiety reactions with accompanying sympathomimetic signs; it is difficult to determine whether this represents a true withdrawal reaction or simply missing the drug effect and an exaggerated return of the symptoms that induced the use of the drug in the first place. In either case, we have found it clinically expedient—even if not always pharmacologically sound—to taper rather than to abruptly withdraw these drugs in markedly dependent patients.

True physical withdrawal syndrome, as evidenced by such symptoms as psychosis or seizures, is rare but has occasionally been documented, even with such long-acting drugs as diazepam; this risk is greater for benzodiazepines with shorter half-lives (e.g., oxazepam, lorazepam, triazolam). With the abuse of shorter-acting benzodiazepines tapering is always reasonable; with longer-acting drugs whose slower elimination makes severe withdrawal reactions less likely, the decision to taper or promptly withdraw remains a clinical one, as indicated earlier. Major criteria for tapering include previous benzodiazepine withdrawal seizures, history of epilepsy, average daily dose > 100 mg diazepam-equivalent.

The degree of dependence must be decided on the basis of history and clinical judgment.

Benzodiazepine Tapering

Once the decision has been made to use tapering therapy for a benzodiazepine-dependent patient, estimate the average daily intake and convert it into an approximate equivalent dose of diazepam (see table on page 37 as a guide). Load to half of this dose by giving 20 mg diazepam q 1-2 hours. In unreliable historians the end-point of loading will not be half the estimated dose but acute symptom reduction and drowsiness.

Tapering should be by 10 mg diazepam per day until a total daily dose of 20 mg is reached and by 5 mg per day thereafter; however, the schedule can be considerably altered by various clinical considerations.

As an example, take a patient who has been ingesting 100 mg of diazepam (or 500 mg of chlordiazepoxide or 20 mg lorazepam) per day. Taper from 50 mg diazepam, with the following daily schedule: 50, 40, 30, 20, 15, 10, 5 mg.

EQUIVALENCE TABLE FOR BENZODIAZEPINES

Benzodiazepine	Common Trade Name	Overall Elimination Rate	Equivalent Dose (mg)
Alprazolam	*(Xanax)*	intermediate	0.25
Bromazepam	*(Lectopam)*	intermediate	3
Chlorazepate	*(Tranxene)*	slow	10
Chlordiazepoxide	*(Librium)*	slow	25
Diazepam	*(Valium)*	slow	5
Flurazepam	*(Dalmane)*	slow	15
Lorazepam	*(Ativan)*	intermediate	1
Oxazepam	*(Serax)*	intermediate to rapid	15
Temazepam	*(Restoril)*	intermediate	10
Triazolam	*(Halcion)*	rapid	0.25

If anxiety and hyperadrenergic symptoms predominate in the withdrawal, beta adrenergic blocking drugs, such as propranolol (40 to 160 mg per day), may be effective additions to the treatment if they are not contraindicated.

NARCOTIC WITHDRAWAL

Narcotic drugs include naturally occurring and synthetically produced opiates and their pharmacological equivalents. Tolerance to these drugs develops rapidly, to the point that a severely dependent individual can take with impunity many times a dose that would be fatal to a novice. Tolerance to the euphoria-producing effect is always greater than to the analgesic effect of these drugs; for this reason patients are able to stay on relatively stable doses for long periods for strictly analgesic purposes.

Most addicts seek euphoria and they use both illicit (e.g., heroin) and legitimate (e.g., morphine, meperidine, oxycodone, etc.) drugs. Hard-core addicts use the drugs intravenously, but many individuals (especially those initiated for medical reasons) manage to maintain their dependence strictly on oral intake. Addicts always run the risk of accidentally overestimating their tolerance (or underestimating the potency of a given drug), which can result in dangerous narcotic overdoses.

Abrupt discontinuation of narcotic intake in physically dependent individuals results in a characteristic withdrawal syndrome, which can be very stormy and unpleasant but, in contrast to hypnosedative withdrawal, is not life-threatening. This fact must be kept in mind when considering various treatment options for narcotic withdrawal.

Narcotic Withdrawal Syndrome

Objective Signs

- Yawning
- Runny nose, sneezing
- Lacrimation

- Dilated pupils
- General vasodilation
- Goose flesh appearing and disappearing repeatedly
- Tachycardia
- Blood pressure elevation
- Respirations slightly increased
- Temperature slightly increased
- Vomiting
- Diarrhea

Subjective Signs

- Anxiety
- Pain in the back, legs, or body
- Bone pain
- Abdominal pain and cramps
- Anorexia

Clinical Judgment Required

- Restlessness, irritability
- Muscle cramps
- Tremor
- Shaking chills

Treatment

Try to establish whether or not the patient is physically dependent on narcotics. Use the following guidelines:

- Drug history
- Urine screen for opiates
- Observing objective signs of withdrawal
- *Naloxone Challenge Test*—This narcotic antagonist should precipitate withdrawal symptoms in addicted individuals who still have the drug aboard. Give 0.4 mg (1 mL) i.v. or 0.8 mg (2 mL) i.m. The effect starts in 1-2 minutes, peaks at 7-10 minutes, and lasts about 30 minutes. Morphine (15 mg) should be kept available to revert a severe reaction. If the patient develops no signs of narcotic withdrawal after

naloxone, he/she is not likely to be physically dependent. However, assessment for psychological dependence and motivation to stop the drug(s) is still required.

If the patient is judged to be physically dependent, the options are as follows:

1. *Do nothing.* Remember "cold turkey" withdrawal is not life-threatening and some addicts find it acceptable. One can always treat unpleasant withdrawal symptoms later, if necessary, by giving a narcotic.

2. *Give a narcotic.* This could be the drug the patient was using or some other commercially available narcotic on which you stabilize the patient according to his/her tolerance and then taper it by approximately 10% per day.

   In institutions where physicians have a methadone licence, the preferred withdrawal method is with *methadone*. The initial dose of methadone is 10-20 mg (empirical), which may be repeated in 12 hours to produce acceptable symptomatic relief; up to 30-40 mg/day may be required. No higher dose is required to control physical signs. Once the daily dose that keeps the patient comfortable has been established, methadone can be given as a single daily dose. Gradually reduce the dose by a fixed percentage, e.g., 10% every 1 or 2 days. In some patients the rate of withdrawal needs to be considerably slower. The administration of methadone in Canada requires a special licence from the Bureau of Dangerous Drugs in Ottawa.

3. *Non-narcotic alternatives.* These usually do not work, e.g., it is generally useless to prescribe benzodiazepines, phenothiazines, or hypnosedatives for narcotic withdrawal. Clonidine (normally prescribed as an antihypertensive), however, has been used as a successful alternative. As a partial alpha adrenergic agonist, it centrally inhibits norepinephrine release, which can produce significant reduction of narcotic withdrawal symptoms.

Clonidine Protocol

Administer 6 μg/kg test dose. If no hypotension occurs:

- 17 μg/kg/day for 10 days, distributed as follows: 7 μg/kg at 8:00 a.m., 3 μg/kg at 3:00 p.m., 7 μg/kg at 10:00 p.m.
- Rapid tapering: 8 μg/kg/day on 11th day, 4 μg/kg/day on 12th day, 2 μg/kg/day on 13th day, none on 14th day.

If diastolic BP is < 60 mm/hg before any dose, omit that dose.

Some Special Problems of Narcotic Withdrawal

Surgery

The pre- and postoperative periods are not the proper times to withdraw addicts from narcotics. They tolerate anaesthesia well but may require larger than usual doses of anaesthetic. The patient's own narcotic or methadone is given during the perioperative period.

Pregnancy

New-born babies of narcotic-addicted mothers will be addicted and will show withdrawal symptoms post-partum; consult a neonatologist. Withdrawal during pregnancy is not desirable because it could produce fetal distress or fetal loss. It is probably best to maintain the pregnant addict on the minimum dose of methadone that keeps her comfortable and plan her withdrawal post-partum.

N.B. For *relative analgesic potencies* of various narcotics, see page 23 (under Narcotic Overdose).

STIMULANT AND PSYCHEDELIC DRUG WITHDRAWAL

The use of these groups of drugs (see Classification, page 13) produces strong psychological dependence and increased tolerance but not physical dependence in the sense that there is no well-defined physical withdrawal syndrome. Abrupt discontinuation of these drugs is therefore permissable.

With stimulant drugs, such as amphetamines, methylphenidate (Ritalin), and cocaine, the major risk is sometimes a profound depression in the withdrawal period after the prolonged use of large doses. Therefore observation of the patient is more important than any pharmacotherapy.

Other drugs (cannabis, LSD, PCP, mescaline, etc.), which have "psychedelic" or hallucinogenic effects, produce more behavioral than toxicological emergencies both during intake and after sudden withdrawal. The patients may present with bizarre, at times dangerously irrational and psychotic, behavior.

Treatment

- Do not be critical. Quiet reassurance is more effective.

- Support and reassurance is sometimes best provided by friends or relatives, who may be encouraged to remain with the patient.

- Take an accurate history re drugs ingested, e.g., he or she may have also taken an overdose of salicylates or another drug.

- Examine the patient and follow vital signs.

- If medication is necessary, give diazepam (20 mg p.o. or 10 mg i.v.) or haloperidol (2-5 mg p.o. or i.m.). Repeat every 1-2 hours if required.

- Chlorpromazine and other phenothiazines may produce untoward interactions with anticholinergics often included in "drugs of abuse" and may produce marked hypotension. Therefore they are best avoided.

• Patients taking drugs intravenously may have regional lymphadenitis, hepatitis, other infections, and occasionally septicemia. Pay attention to these possibilities.

POLY-DRUG AND COMBINATION DRUG WITHDRAWAL

In the preceding chapters we have considered management issues re withdrawal of various drugs as if they were always used singly. But many patients, of course, abuse varying combinations of substances. This is sometimes difficult to sort out because the histories, the doses, the frequency of administration, etc. are in many cases notoriously uncertain. Toxicology tests can be quite helpful in these situations. Even after a diligent effort to obtain an accurate history (from the patient and other informants) and toxicology tests, there will still be a certain number of cases in which, at best, only an educated guess can be made as to what was used and which substance is the most important clinically.

As a general principle, if two or more drugs have been significantly abused, we recommend the withdrawal of one at a time and maintaining the other(s). First, start withdrawing the drug that potentially represents the most problems. For example, in narcotic-hypnosedative combination abuse, withdraw the hypnotic (phenobarb-loading technique) and maintain the patient on the narcotic; start tapering the latter when the hypnotic withdrawal is out of the way. The same would apply to alcohol-narcotic withdrawal. In cases of combined alcohol-benzodiazepine abuse, alcohol withdrawal is the priority; in fact, administration of a benzodiazepine is part of the treatment anyway, but in such cases diazepam loading may have to be followed by diazepam tapering (see page 36). Patients with combined alcohol-hypnosedative dependence may be a problem. They may need to be phenobarbital loaded, supplemented by a judicious use of oral diazepam, but the usual guidelines of diazepam loading would not apply because judging the effects of the two drugs would be confounding. In cases of combined dependence on hynosedatives and benzodiazepines, the hypnosedative withdrawal (phenobarb loading) takes priority and might be all that will be required.

It needs to be emphasized that there are no firm rules to cover all eventualities. Clinical judgment, combined with some elementary knowledge of pharmacological principles, will guide you through most situations.

Another related problem involves those commercial drug preparations that contain more than one ingredient. One *must* always know what is in a drug the patient has been taking, regardless of which ingredient's effect he or she was seeking. For example, the patient taking large doses of Percodan may be after the narcotic effect, but the physician must realize that the patient is also ingesting a lot of ASA with it. Or the person abusing Fiorinal-C will be on ASA, codeine, and barbiturate; he/she may have taken it for analgesia but the major problem will be barbiturate withdrawal. Below is a selected list of commercial combination drugs that are most commonly abused by patients.

222	= ASA + caffeine + codeine 8 mg
282	= ASA + caffeine + codeine 15 mg
292	= ASA + caffeine + codeine 30 mg
294	= ASA + caffeine + codeine 65 mg
282 MEP	= see 282 + meprobamate 200 mg
293	= see 292 + 30 mg slow release codeine (Total Codeine: 60 mg)
692	= ASA + caffeine + propoxyphene 65 mg
Darvon-N	= ASA + caffeine + propoxyphene 100 mg
Fiorinal	= ASA + caffeine + butalbital 50 mg
Fiorinal-C	= see Fiorinal + codeine 15 mg (C$^1/_4$) or 30 mg (C$^1/_2$)
Novahistex-C	= codeine 15 mg + phenylephrine + diphenylpyraline (per 5 mL)
Novahistex-DH	= hydrocodone 5 mg + phenylephrine + diphenylpyraline (per 5 mL)
Percocet	= oxycodone 4.5 mg + acetaminophen + caffeine
Percodan	= oxycodone 4.5 mg + ASA + caffeine
Percodan-Demi	= oxycodone 2.25 mg + ASA + caffeine
Tuinal	= secobarbital + amobarbital (100 or 200 mg)
Tussionex	= hydrocodone 5 mg + phenyltoloxamine
Tylenol No. 1	= acetaminophen + caffeine + codeine 8 mg
Tylenol No. 2	= acetaminophen + caffeine + codeine 15 mg
Tylenol No. 3	= acetaminophen + caffeine + codeine 30 mg
Tylenol No. 4	= acetaminophen + caffeine + codeine 60 mg

CHRONIC PAIN AND DRUG ABUSE

It is almost always difficult to determine why an individual uses drugs; the answers to this question are frequently elusive. There is, however, a group of people who will give a very clearcut reason: chronic pain (e.g., headache, low back pain, or other). These patients make up a sizeable proportion of those whom we lump together as abusers of *prescription drugs*. This term does not include illicitly obtained licit drugs but is confined to those that are acquired directly through physicians' prescriptions. The majority of patients who use drugs secondary to chronic pain are exclusively prescription drug abusers. The supplier is sometimes a single physician, but in many cases patients employ the multiple prescription technique, using several doctors.

We face two immediate issues with these patients: (1) to withdraw the drug and (2) to offer an alternative for the control of pain. The first is easy, the second is exceedingly difficult. Many patients say that they are not "drug addicts" and that they will be glad to give up their drug as long as somebody can solve their pain problem.

The skillfully taken history will suggest something about the patient's motivation. Many patients pay at least lip service to the necessity of stopping the drug; further probing, however, may reveal that the real motivating force may be outside pressure (e.g., family) or the refusal of the physician to supply the prescription (often the same physician who has been issuing it for years). Physical examination and subsequent investigation may or may not reveal a cause for the patient's pain; in many cases it does not.

Eventually these patients can be classified as belonging to one of the following categories:

1. Those with defineable organic disease for whom the continuation of the "abused" drug is justifiable. Dose adjustments may still be needed. It is important to recognize that in our zeal to stamp out the abuse of prescription drugs we should not deprive patients who legitimately need them.

2. Those who eventually admit that pain is not the real issue; they use pain as an excuse to obtain the prescriptions.

3. Those who have a proven or at least likely cause for their pain but have been treated with inappropriate drugs that lead to drug dependence (e.g., narcotics for migraine, osteoarthritis, etc.).

4. Those for whom no amount of probing or investigation turns up a reasonable cause for the pain, yet we are convinced that the patient is not "faking" it and that he/she truly suffers. These patients are often said to have "psychogenic pain."

In all but the first category, the abused drug(s) should be discontinued. Whether or not to stop the drug abruptly or to institute one of the withdrawal regimes described earlier must be decided. Keep in mind the potential problems created by combination drugs or poly-drug abuse (see page 41).

In addition to the withdrawal of the offending drug, the physician should make an attempt to clarify the nature of the alleged pain and should initiate an alternative drug treatment when this seems reasonable (e.g., ergotamine or beta-blockers for migraine, anti-inflammatory drugs for arthritis, etc.) or offer a non-pharmacological alternative (e.g., relaxation therapy, psycho-therapy, etc.). Finding such an alternative represents the only chance for many patients to avoid returning to their former pattern of drug use. However, it is not unreasonable to propose to patients that they may have to learn to put up with a certain amount of discomfort as a trade-off for avoiding drug dependence.

MEDICAL COMPLICATIONS

MEDICAL COMPLICATIONS

The potential medical problems associated with alcohol and drug use are numerous and often complex. While representatives of various professions may be involved in a patient's recovery process, the medical complications must be dealt with by physicians. Restoration of physical health is usually a prerequisite to rehabilitation.

Patients using alcohol and other drugs may have the same diseases as those who are not users. The natural history of coincidental illness is, however, frequently affected by their use of alcohol and drugs and by their lifestyle. The types of illness found in these patients, of course, encompass the entire spectrum of medicine, but certain medical problems more predominantly represent direct or indirect complications from alcohol or drug use. Detailed discussion of these complications is beyond the scope of this short handbook, but in this section we look at some of the diseases that must be considered in patients who have alcohol- and drug-related problems. For in-depth information, however, the appropriate textbooks should be consulted.

MEDICAL COMPLICATIONS RELATED TO ALCOHOL

Neurological Complications Related to Alcohol

Wernicke-Korsakoff Syndrome

This syndrome is characterized by the Wernicke triad (confusion, ataxia, and ophthalmoplegia) and Korsakoff psychosis (severe recent memory impairment associated with confabulation). In its most florid form the syndrome has some mortality, while subclinical forms of the disease may go unrecognized. Thiamine deficiency has a prominent role in this syndrome. The prophylactic administration of at least a single parenteral dose of thiamine (50-100 mg) is well justified in every patient sick enough to require hospital admission for alcohol-related problems. In cases of established Wernicke-Korsakoff syndrome, the Wernicke component usually responds well to thiamine therapy whereas the Korsakoff part does not.

Peripheral Neuropathy

Peripheral neuropathy is also largely associated with thiamine deficiency and possibly other nutritional deficiencies. It is a symmetrical, initially distal, sensorimotor neuropathy affecting the legs more than the arms and later it spreads proximally. Loss of ankle-jerk is often an early clinical sign.

Cerebral Atrophy

Cerebral atrophy in heavy alcohol users affects the cortex more than the ventricles. A certain degree of reversibility has been demonstrated with abstinence. The clinical "organic brain syndrome" that is associated with brain atrophy can range from minimal cognitive and intellectual impairment to severe dementia.

Cerebellar Degeneration

Related to alcohol use this degeneration mainly involves the vermis and the main clinical correlate of this is ataxic gait. Other cerebellar functions such as tone and co-ordination (e.g., finger-nose test) may be relatively preserved.

Pseudo-Parkinsonism

Pseudo-Parkinsonism in alcohol-dependent individuals has been well documented; any or all of the Parkinsonian symptoms (tremor, rigidity, bradykinesia) may be present, but they resolve spontaneously with abstinence.

Subdural Hematoma

More likely to occur in this population than in any other, subdural hematoma results from relatively trivial (or unnoticed) head injury because of "stretched" subdural veins in patients with cortical atrophy. A high index of suspicion is warranted in any patient with headache, intellectual deterioration, unexplained drowsiness, or a bizarre neurological picture. Remember that symptoms can fluctuate in subdural hematoma and that signs of raised intracranial pressure are rare. When in doubt, order a CT scan.

Gastroenterological Complications Related to Alcohol

Alcoholic Liver Diseases

Among the most common complications related to heavy drinking, three distinct but often overlapping diseases come under this grouping:

- Fatty liver, which is the most common hepatic response to alcohol; in most cases it causes no clinical problems and is readily reversible with abstinence.
- Alcoholic hepatitis which can range from a clinically asymptomatic disease to a florid acute illness with fever, jaundice, abdominal pain, and death.
- Cirrhosis, in a pathological sense, is an end-stage irreversible disease, but clinically it can be stable and latent—especially in abstinent individuals—or it can be an incapacitating and life-threatening illness with ascites, portal hypertension, and hepatic encephalopathy.

Neither the clinical picture nor laboratory tests can reliably predict which of these alcoholic liver conditions are present; only liver biopsy can make the distinction with any certainty. With regard to laboratory tests, it is well to remember that aminotrasferases are usually only mildly elevated and AST/ALT ratio is > 1, often > 2 (in contrast to viral hepatitis). Enzyme values do not correlate with prognosis. Indicators of poor prognosis are persistent jaundice, decreased albumin, prolonged prothrombin time, and anemia.

Alcoholic Gastritis and Esophagitis

These conditions are responsible for dyspeptic symptoms as well as for acute and chronic blood loss. *Peptic ulcer* is probably not any more common in

48

heavy alcohol users than in the general population, but its complications may be adversely affected by alcohol. When treating dyspeptic symptoms or peptic ulcer disease in these patients, a few points must be remembered:

- If H_2 receptor blockers are used ranitidine may have some advantages over cimetidine; it is less likely to cause confusion, does not produce gynecomastia (which may be an important issue in those with alcoholic liver disease or on spironolactone therapy), and it does not inhibit hepatic microsomal enzymes, therefore, the toxicity of concurrently used (and abused) drugs is not augmented.

- Sucralfate is a locally acting cytoprotective polysaccharide with no or minimal systemic effects; it is an effective alternative to H_2 blockers in the treatment of peptic ulcer.

- Many currently available antacids have low sodium content (< 1 mg/ 5 mL) and are thus acceptable for patients with alcoholic liver disease who require restricted sodium intake.

Alcoholic Pancreatitis

Alcoholic pancreatitis consists of acute attacks superimposed on a chronic inflammatory process (chronic relapsing pancreatitis) or of a progressive chronic inflammatory destruction of the pancreas without acute attacks (chronic pancreatitis). In either case, the eventual end result may be exocrine pancreatic insufficiency with or without diabetes; for clinically significant steatorrhea to occur, > 90% of exocrine pancreas needs to be destroyed. The acute attack presents mainly with pain.

This diagnosis should be considered in any patient with acute upper abdominal pain in the appropriate clinical setting. Pancreatic pain is typically worse in recumbency, relieved by sitting up. Rigidity is not usually marked and there is a varying degree of ileus. In the most severe cases there is shock, hemoconcentration, and acute renal failure.

Diagnosis is largely clinical. Serum amylase is usually elevated early, but remember that it is also frequently elevated in cases of perforated viscus, mesenteric occlusion, bowel obstruction, salpingitis, etc. On the other hand, patients with marked chronic pancreatitis may not have elevated serum amylase during an acute attack. Amylase clearance/creatinine clearance ratio has been suggested as fairly specific for pancreatitis (normal, approximately 3%; in pancreatitis, 5% or >). Other possibly helpful but not specific diagnostic tests include pancreatic calcifications on plain film (suggest underlying chronic pancreatitis), elevated left hemidiaphragm, pleural effusion, peritoneal effusion (↑amylase concentration), hypocalcemia. If in doubt, obtain surgical consultation; acute pancreatitis attack is not a surgical condition but one must be certain that this is the condition that the patient has.

In the management of acute attacks pain relief is most important; meperidine (Demerol) 100 mg q 3-4 hours prn is preferable to morphine, which may cause spasm of the sphincter of Oddi. Fluids and electrolytes need to be replaced. Pancreatic secretion can be decreased during the acute pain by giving nothing p.o. and—at least in those patients who have nausea and vomiting—by nasogastric suction. Pancreatic enzyme replacement therapy may be required in patients with severe exocrine insufficiency.

Hematological Complications Related to Alcohol

Anemia

The *anemias* in heavy users of alcohol are frequently complex, multifactorial, and difficult to sort out. Keep in mind that alcohol per se can cause macrocytosis (see page 7), which may confound the investigation in as much as cell-size (as an index of anemia) is concerned. Iron deficiency is common, secondary to bleeding from gastritis, esophageal varices, etc.; nonetheless the alcoholic iron-deficient patient deserves the same investigation as anyone else. (Remember that alcohol does not immunize against cancer of the colon.) Folate deficiency anemia is quite common because of poor diet or interference by alcohol with folate absorption and utilization. Vitamin B_{12} deficiency is rare, except in advanced pancreatic disease (failure to split B_{12}-R protein complex). Sideroblastic anemia (ring sideroblasts in bone marrow) is attributed to inhibition of pyridoxal phosphate by alcohol. Decreased RBC survival (with or without associated leukopenia and thrombocytopenia) can be caused by hypersplenism secondary to liver disease and portal hypertension.

Anemias of any etiology, during and after investigation of the cause, should be diligently treated, trying to bring Hgb level to > 100 g/L. Especially in patients with liver disease, the restoration of Hgb to acceptable levels is not only beneficial for the anemia itself but also for the liver because a relative hypoxia of the liver may have a role in alcoholic liver disease.

Toxic Thrombocytopenia

Toxic thrombocytopenia due to alcohol intoxication can be quite profound and occasionally symptomatic (e.g., petecchiae); it is due to alcohol-induced inhibition of megakaryocyte function. In contrast to the thrombocytopenia of hypersplenism, the toxic variety is rapidly reversible with abstinence (sometimes with an "overshoot").

Leukocytosis

With this finding one should search for infection. Remember though, that patients with hypersplenism will not be able to mount this response to infection; on the other hand, alcoholic hepatitis by itself can produce leukocytosis.

Endocrine and Metabolic Complications Related to Alcohol

Sexual Dysfunction

This condition commonly accompanies alcohol dependence. Hypoandrogenism in males is more common in those who have liver disease but may be caused by alcohol itself. While alcohol may remove sexual inhibitions, impotence is common, i.e., ". . . it provokes the desire, but takes away the performance." (Shakespeare: Macbeth)

Pseudo-Cushing Syndrome

Pseudo-Cushing syndrome refers to transient cushingoid features, as the result of stimulation of the pituitary-adrenal axis by prolonged and excessive use of alcohol. The syndrome disappears with abstinence.

Diabetes

Diabetes may be secondary to advanced chronic pancreatic disease; severe liver disease may also cause glucose intolerance. Needless to say diabetes mellitus, which is coincidental to alcoholism, may present serious management problems in non-compliant heavy users of alcohol.

Hyperuricemia

A metabolic consequence of alcoholic oxidation, hyperuricemia frequently accompanies heavy alcohol intake. Clinically, this may be of importance in those individuals who have gout.

Alcoholic Hypoglycemia and Ketoacidosis

These are somewhat interrelated metabolic abnormalities, which from time to time present emergency management problems. They occur in a setting of excessive alcohol intake *plus* starvation. The latter depletes glycogen stores to which the normal compensatory response would be increased gluconeogenesis. Alcohol, however, inhibits gluconeogenesis and the net result may be hypoglycemia which sometimes may be symptomatic, requiring treatment (50 mL 50% glucose).

The response to untreated hypoglycemia is the cessation of insulin secretion and the production of counter-regulatory hormones. The latter, apart from a tendency to increase blood sugar, will mobilize free fatty acids, which will be incompletely metabolized to ketoacids in the liver. The characteristics of the resulting alcoholic ketoacidosis are the following:

- Female predominance (for unknown reasons)
- History of ETOH + starvation ± vomiting
- Anion-gap type of metabolic acidosis (mainly due to ↑ beta-hydroxy-butyrate)
- Normoglycemia or mild hyperglycemia

Keep in mind that the urinary nitroprusside (Acetest) test does not pick up beta-hydroxy-butyrate, thus one cannot rely on this test to judge the degree of ketosis. Apart from blood gases and blood sugar, order determination of ketones (and lactate) in blood when metabolic acidosis occurs in alcoholics. Alcoholic ketoacidosis is usually self-correcting with resumption of feeding; if any i.v. treatment is required it is usually glucose. Not infrequently there is a metabolic alkalosis associated with alcoholic ketoacidosis in those patients who have had antecedent protracted vomiting. In such cases NaCl (+ K) often needs to be added to the treatment.

Cardiorespiratory Complications Related to Alcohol

Cardiomyopathy and Dysrhythmias

Excessive alcohol consumption can depress myocardial function and produce pump failure; strictly speaking, this would constitute *alcoholic cardiomyopathy*. Various atrial and ventricular dysrhythmias are frequently associated with excessive alcohol intake or with severe withdrawal. Thus alcohol use must be considered in the differential diagnosis of patients presenting with otherwise unexplained heart failure or dysrhythmias. The clue to "alcoholic heart disease" is that it is associated with heavy alcohol intake, disappears with abstinence (this reversibility is lost in advanced stages), and that other causes of heart disease can be reasonably excluded. It is well to remember that sudden death, secondary to alcoholic dysrhythmias, has been reported. The best treatment of alcoholic heart disease is abstinence, aided by the usual measures, e.g., verapamil for PAT, digitalization for rapid atrial fibrillation, lidocaine for ventricular dysrhythmias, etc.

Hypertension

Hypertension is said to be somewhat associated with alcoholism according to some epidemiological studies, but the clinical relevance of this is uncertain. Unquestionably, many patients are transiently hypertensive in the alcohol withdrawal period due to excessive catecholamine release. These patients, however, usually do not require treatment for hypertension. We suggest that the presence of frank hypertension past the withdrawal period be established (and then the usual basic investigation carried out) before declaring the patient hypertensive and committing him or her to lifelong treatment.

Obstructive Sleep Apnoea

Obstructive sleep apnoea precipitated and aggravated by alcohol has been recently recognized. The periodic anoxia associated with sleep apnoea could play a role in insults to the brain, liver, and heart.

Ischemic Heart Disease

This is probably not more common in heavy drinkers than in the general population (alcohol has even been postulated to have a coronary-protective effect via ↑high-density lipoprotein). If morbidity of ischemic heart disease is not adversely affected by alcohol, mortality risk might be (for example, via arrhythmogenic effects or sleep apnoea).

Infections and Alcohol

In heavy drinkers there is increased incidence of all kinds of infections because of (1) ↓ WBC function, (2) immunologic factors, (3) lifestyle. Two particularly common problems deserve special mention.

Pneumonia

The pneumonias are most often caused by common organisms (e.g., streptococcus pneumoniae). However, bacteria that are rare pathogens in others are relatively more common causes of disease in alcohol-dependent patients, e.g., Klebsiella (upper lobe), anaerobes.

Bacterial Peritonitis

Spontaneous bacterial peritonitis in patients with ascites is a potentially devastating complication of alcoholic liver disease. Clinical signs and symptoms are abdominal pain, tenderness, rebound tenderness, and fever. Remember that all of these do not have to be present, but this condition should be suspected in any patient with ascites who has even one of these signs or symptoms. In this case—and if there is no contraindication—perform a diagnostic tap (WBC count, differential, pH, gram stain, culture) and order a blood culture. Presumptive evidence of spontaneous bacterial peritonitis is provided by WBC $> 500/mm_3$ or polymorphs $> 250/mm_3$ in ascitic fluid; ascitic pH < 7.30 in the absence of systemic acidosis. Confirmation is by finding the offending micro-organism. Most common pathogen is E. coli, but many bacteria can cause it (anaerobes, conspicuously rarely). "Blind" treatment should be started on the basis of clinical suspicion and/or presumptive laboratory evidence (see above). Ampicillin (plus an aminoglycoside in very ill patients) is usually a good starting therapy, altered later if necessary, based on culture results.

Carcinogenic Effect of Alcohol

The carcinogenic effect of alcohol use is based on epidemiological evidence. Increased incidence of mouth, pharyngeal, laryngeal, and esophageal cancer and hepatoma has been reported in heavy drinkers. Keep in mind that cigarette smoking is very prevalent in this population, but alcohol may act as a co-carcinogen.

Fetal Alcohol Syndrome (FAS) and Fetal Alcohol Effects (FAE)

Possible embryologic effects of alcohol have not been recognized until relatively recently. The following have been associated with the FAS and FAE:

- Mental deficiency
- Irritability
- Reduced body weight and length
- Hypotonia, poor motor co-ordination

- Microcephaly
- Facial abnormalities:

    short palpebral fissures

    upturned nose

    depressed nasal bridge

    smooth filtrum

    thin upper lip

    epicanthal folds

    small jaw

There are still unresolved and controversial issues re incidence, magnitude of risk, correlation with quantity of consumption, etc. Nonetheless, there is little doubt that the possibility of the syndrome is real. Everything should be done to assure abstinence in pregnant women.

MEDICAL COMPLICATIONS OF DRUG ABUSE

Infections and Drug Abuse

Viral Hepatitis

Viral hepatitis, especially Hepatitis B, is a relatively common complication of intravenous drug abuse. The clinical spectrum is variable, ranging from asymptomatic to fulminant cases. The majority of cases are thought to be anicteric. Recovery is the rule in most patients, but there is a risk of chronicity (sometimes ending in cirrhosis and/or hepatoma) in a sizeable minority (the latter does not occur with Hepatitis A).

Laboratory Procedures and Treatment

- Complete evaluation of liver function should be done in all suspected cases; the progression or regression of the disease should be followed by regular biochemical monitoring. AST/ALT (SGOT/SGPT) ratio is usually < 1 in viral hepatitis in contrast to alcoholic liver disease (> 1 or 2). The absolute value of these aminotransferase enzymes is usually much higher in viral hepatitis than in alcoholic liver disease.

- Serological diagnosis in suspected cases should begin with testing for two serologic markers: HB_s Ag (evidence of Hepatitis B) and anti-HAV I_gM (evidence of Hepatitis A). HB_s Ag-positive cases should have their e-antigen and anti-e status determined (e-antigen correlates with infectivity).

- In all previously HB_s Ag-positive cases, repeat the test 3-6 months later, even after apparent clinical recovery, to rule out chronicity or carrier state. Test also for HB_s Ab—its presence indicates acquired immunity. In HB$_S$ Ag-positive carriers e-antigen is a reasonably good marker of chronicity and/or infectivity.

- Bed rest or activity is determined by the patient's tolerance during acute illness. Excessive activity is to be avoided.

- A well-balanced normal diet (up to 3000 calories) is given as tolerated.

- Corticosteroids are not to be given even in the most severe cases of acute viral hepatitis.

- For Hepatitis B "blood precautions" and not enteric isolation procedures are required; the latter is applied only in cases of proven Hepatitis A (positive for anti-HAV I$_g$M) or if the patient with Hepatitis B has hematochezia.

Immunoprophylaxis

- Ordinary immune-globulin (gamma globulin) has prophylactic value in close household contacts of patients with Hepatitis A.

- Hepatitis B immune-globulin (high titer of anti-HB$_S$) is a prophylactic agent for passive immunization in cases of intimate (e.g., sexual) exposure to Hepatitis B patients or accidental (e.g., needleprick) exposure to their blood.

- Hepatitis B vaccine (active immunization) is available to "high risk" individuals, e.g., selected health care personnel, hemodialysis patients, blood bank workers, laboratory technicians, homosexually active males, prostitutes, and users of illicit injectable drugs.

- Physicians who are often exposed to blood (e.g., residents, interns) are at relatively high risk and it is recommended that they be vaccinated against Hepatitis B.

The viral hepatitis field is very rapidly changing and developing and the literature should be closely followed. One new development is a test for I$_g$M antibody to Hepatitis B core antigen (anti-HBC I$_g$M), which should be commercially available soon. It is an accurate serologic marker of Hepatitis B infection. It is particularly useful in the "window period" or gap between the disappearance of HB$_S$ Ag and the appearance HB$_S$ Ab.

Another new development is the recognition of delta agent hepatitis, a newly documented hepatitis caused by a unique virus that requires Hepatitis B virus for replication; delta hepatitis only infects patients who are HB$_S$ Ag positive. It can cause acute and chronic hepatitis in HB$_S$ Ag carriers. In North America intravenous drug abusers are thought to be the main targets for delta hepatitis infection. The diagnosis can be suggested by finding anti-delta antibodies in the serum, for which an assay is expected to be available in the near future.

AIDS

AIDS (acquired immuno-deficiency syndrome) is mentioned here for two reasons: (1) it is caused by a virus (HTLV-III) and (2) after homosexual males (75%) the second largest group at risk is reported to be i.v. drug users (15%). These two groups are, of course, not mutually exclusive. The syndrome is new, still rare, but reported to increase exponentially, with a doubling of cases every 7 to 8 months. The main features of AIDS include T-lymphocyte defect ($\downarrow$helper/suppressor cell ratio), fever, malaise, lymphadenopathy, opportunistic infections (Pneumocystis carinii, candida, mycobacteria, CMV, etc.), Kaposi-sarcoma, and a high fatality rate.

There is some resistance by health care staff to accept Hepatitis B vaccination mainly on the basis of fear that the vaccine may be a vehicle for transmitting the AIDS agent. There is no evidence to support this. So far no known occurrence of AIDS nor transmission of any other infection has been associated with the Hepatitis B vaccine; it is highly unlikely that any infectious agent could survive the physical and chemical procedures required for the production of the vaccine.

Bacterial Infections

- Cellulitis, particularly of staphylococcal or streptococcal origin, at the site of injections in i.v. drug users is common.

- Bacterial endocarditis of i.v. drug users has an estimated incidence of 1 to 3 in 1000. Men are at more risk than women. All organisms that cause natural valve endocarditis may be the causative agent in i.v. drug users, but there are some peculiarities among the latter population, e.g., staphylococcus aureus—rare in the general population—is a common cause of endocarditis among i.v. users; there is a tendency to affect the tricuspid valve. Prognosis is good if treated promptly.

Pulmonary Complications of Drug Abuse

- *Talcosis and granulomas* (due to adulterant).

- *Heroin-addicts' pulmonary edema* ($\uparrow$permeability of pulmonary capillaries caused by opiates). Naloxone reverses the process.

Renal Complications of Drug Abuse

- *Heroin nephropathy*—focal glomerulosclerosis leading to renal failure (reported mainly in Blacks so far).

- *Analgesic nephropathy*—secondary to chronic abuse of ASA, phenacetin, or combination analgesics. Initially an interstitial (tubular) defect, which eventually may lead to renal failure.

56

Glue Sniffers' Encephalopathy

- Cerebellar symptoms predominant, plus impaired intellectual function.

Drug Psychoses

- Bizarre behavior, schizophrenia-like symptoms, etc. associated with amphetamines, PCP, hallucinogenics, etc. Consider the possibility of severe rebound depression after discontinuation of amphetamines.

Section
VI

TREATMENT OF
SUBSTANCE-USING
BEHAVIOR

58

TREATMENT OF SUBSTANCE-USING BEHAVIOR

The ultimate goal in the treatment of alcohol- and drug-abusing patients is to assist them in acknowledging their problem and then to help alter the destructive elements in lifestyle to maintain an improved state of physical, mental, and social well-being. It is not sufficient to work only with the medical problems involved; in most instances the problems associated with alcohol/drug use pervade every part of the individual's lifestyle, which means that all aspects of his/her biopsychosocial status must be addressed.

Nonetheless, the first and essential part of treatment involves detoxification and management of withdrawal and medical complications, which is the major thrust of this handbook. The physician has no options vis-à-vis these issues; no other professional group is qualified to do this job.

The next—and more difficult—phase is long-term management and rehabili-tation. At our present level of knowledge, it is somewhat presumptuous to call this treatment because what we are really doing is helping the patient in his/her attempts to recover spontaneously. Physicians are but one of several professional groups potentially involved in this process. It is incumbent upon those who don't wish to actively participate in this undertaking to refer the patient to someone who does. It may be helpful to use an existing addiction-specific rehabilitation service or to involve staff working in other disciplines (e.g., social work, psychology, nursing, occupational therapy, clergy, etc.). Discussion of the various available rehabilitation programs is beyond the scope of this handbook, but a partial listing of available assessment/referral and detoxification centres in Ontario follows this section as an appendix.

We have singled out three issues, however, which should be of particular interest to physicians and are therefore discussed in this section. One is the use of anti-alcohol drugs, the second is the involvement of the patient's family, and the third, the problem of our drug- or alcohol-dependent colleague.

THE ANTI-ALCOHOL DRUGS

While long-term recovery from alcohol dependence is largely aided by socio-behavioral counselling and other supportive means, physicians have a relatively specific pharmacological aid at their disposal: the prescription of such anti-alcohol drugs as disulfiram (Antabuse) and calcium carbimide (Temposil). These are also called alcohol-sensitizing drugs, protective drugs, or deterrent drugs, depending on one's perception of their effect. While their overall efficacy in the management of alcohol dependence is still uncertain, undoubtedly there is a subgroup of patients who may benefit from their use.

The effect of anti-alcohol drugs is based on their inhibition of alcohol metabolism at the acetaldehyde level; the accumulating acetaldehyde pro-duces an unpleasant reaction, consisting of flushing, choking, chest oppres-sion, nausea-vomiting, tachycardia, and hypotension. The person taking these drugs knows that he/she cannot take a drink without producing this reaction; this should be a sufficient deterrent against impulsive drinking and insurance for the maintenance of abstinence in those who have made a serious decision about it. If a reaction does occur, general supportive measures are usually sufficient (supine position, O_2). In case of profound hypotension, vasopressor agents (e.g., dopamine) may be needed.

Disulfiram and its metabolites are long acting and the drug needs to be discontinued for several days before there is no longer a risk of reaction with alcohol; calcium carbimide's effects are much shorter and, if drinking does take place, the reaction is often less pronounced than with disulfiram. The drugs are contraindicated in patients hypersensitive to them and in those unable to comprehend their use; other contraindications include heart disease (mainly because of the risk of hypotension during a reaction), psychosis, severe liver disease, and severe neuropathy (for more details see table on page 61).

The dose of disulfiram is 250 mg once a day, preferably at bedtime. Calcium carbimide is given in 50-mg doses b.i.d. The latter drug is prescribed to patients who cannot tolerate disulfiram and also as a short-term protection for certain risky occasions. A full explanation should be given to all patients.

Some reasons for stopping treatment include an improvement in the patient's status, the resumption of drinking, noncompliance, missed appointments, pregnancy, and changes in liver or cardiac function.

DIFFERENCES BETWEEN THE TWO DRUGS IN ENZYME INHIBITION

ENZYME	DISULFIRAM	CALCIUM CARBIMIDE
Aldehyde dehydrogenese		
— Type of inhibition:	IRREVERSIBLE	REVERSIBLE
— Onset of inhibition:	12 hours	within 1 hour
— Duration of inhibition:	more than 6 days	up to 24 hours
Dopamine-β-Hydroxylase	INHIBITED	NOT INHIBITED
Hepatic Mixed-Function Oxidases	INHIBITED	NOT INHIBITED

SIDE EFFECTS AND TOXICITY THAT MIGHT OCCUR
DURING TREATMENT

CLINICAL MANIFESTATIONS	DISULFIRAM	CALCIUM CARBIMIDE
1. Medical complications during acetaldehyde-mediated reactions	yes	yes
2. Drug-induced toxicity		
Behavioral toxicity		
drowsiness, lethargy	yes	no
depression	possible	no
psychosis	possible	no
Neurotoxicty		
neuropathy	yes	no
Hepatoxicity		
abnormal liver function tests	yes	not reported
hepatitis	yes	not reported
hepatocytic inclusion bodies	yes	yes
Metabolic toxicity		
increased cholesterol	yes	no
anti-thyroid action	no	in animals only
Neuroendocrine toxicity	yes	no
Teratogenic effects	yes	not reported
3. Drug-drug interactions (drugs undergoing oxidative metabolism)	yes	no

CONTRAINDICATIONS OF ANTI-ALCOHOL DRUGS

CLINICAL CONDITION	DISULFIRAM	CALCIUM CARBIMIDE
Myocardial disorders		
angina	a	a
coronary artery disease	a	a
cardiac arrhythmias	a	a
cardiomyopathy	a	a
Severe pulmonary insufficiency and asthma	a	b
Advanced liver disease		
acute hepatitis	a	b
cirrhosis with ascites	a	b
Thyroid disease	—	b
Chronic renal disorders	a	b
Neuropsychiatric disorders		
depression	a	b
functional psychosis	a	b
toxic psychosis	a	a
neuropathy	a	b
Requiring treatment with other drugs that undergo oxidative metabolism	b	—
Severe personality disorders, characterized		
by loss of impulse control	a	a
by depression with risk of suicide	a	a
Inability or unwillingness to attend regular follow-up clinics	a	a
Pregnancy	a	a
History of adverse drug reaction	a	a

a — absolute contraindication
b — relative contraindication

FAMILY INVOLVEMENT

When considering possible avenues of treatment, consideration should be given to the entire family. For purposes of personal survival, family members normally assume behavior patterns that maintain a homeostasis in the system. A distorted balance, as occurs when one member starts becoming dependent on a chemical, can cause psychological and/or biological symptoms in the other family members. This distortion will lead to problems within each individual as well as with the functioning of the family as a unit.

Individual family members may, in an effort to protect the dependent person, unwittingly act as "enablers," perpetuating the dependence. In order for recovery to take place the behavior of the dependent person needs to be identified and then rectified.

Both the spouse and the children of the chemically dependent patient may have a high incidence and wide range of physical and psychiatric problems. These might include headaches, asthma, minor gastrointestinal disorders, high incidence of trauma, anxiety, insomnia, depression, frequent upper respiratory infections—the list is lengthy.

Children of problem drinkers almost need to be considered as a special group. The incidence of alcohol/drug use in these children as adults is markedly higher than in the general population. While still children, they may exhibit many behavioral problems. Common ones include school difficulties such as truancy, poor scholastic performance, and acting out behavior. These children may also be compulsive overachievers. One child may take on a parental role to care for the others. Poor socializing skills may emerge—the child becoming a loner or developing socially unacceptable behavior.

All of these considerations must be taken into account when considering treatment for the alcohol- and/or drug-dependent patient. Marital/family therapy may be an extremely important component of treatment. Even if the person is not ready to accept help, the various other family members may benefit from some form of assistance such as counselling or attending Al-Anon or Alateen meetings.

PROGRAM FOR DOCTORS ON CHEMICALS

The program, Doctors on Chemicals, was started in 1977 to explore the problem of dependence among physicians. A number of initiatives have been taken to learn more about the nature and causes of this problem, and particular attention has been given to early recognition and treatment. Research and educational activities have been stimulated to help physicians avoid problems of alcohol or drug use. The profession has responded to these activities by taking more interest in these problems; more doctors are seeking help for themselves and for their colleagues. This in turn has resulted in the development of better methods of assessment and new initiatives for treatment and rehabilitation.

How Many Doctors Misuse Alcohol or Drugs?

It has been estimated that the incidence of alcohol dependence among physicians in general may be as high as 10%, and there is no reason to believe that doctors in Ontario are any less vulnerable. While it is more difficult to estimate the number of physicians who are drug dependent, doctors are probably more at risk than the general population because of their access to drugs. If we accept 10% as a conservative estimate, there are at least 1,500 doctors in Ontario with a dependence on alcohol and other drugs.

How Can You Tell if There Is a Problem?

Problems relating to the use of alcohol and drugs, like other problems, come in different shapes and sizes. A well-established dependence, which affects the conduct and behavior of a physician in the office or at the hospital, will likely be spotted by colleagues and patients. Earlier stages of dependence are not so easily recognized.

Any self-administration of narcotic or controlled drugs, other than in an acute emergency when another physician is not available, is a misuse. If the physician has been self-prescribing such medication in increasing quantities over a period of months, it may be assumed that a dependence has been established.

The person consuming hazardous amounts of alcohol may have a variety of problems (see page 9). A physician's failure to control his or her drinking, a gradual withdrawal from family members and friends, a disinterest in professional and community affairs, charges of impaired driving, and other examples of irresponsible behavior are characteristic signs of a dependence which should not be ignored.

It is important to recognize physicians with alcohol- and drug-related problems and for them to receive treatment as early as possible. Those with a well-established dependence can be expected to deny it. They usually recognize that they have a problem but may be either unwilling or unable to give up the chemical. Unless they receive help, physicians frequently continue to hurt themselves and those who are close to them and may present a risk to their patients.

What Help Is Available?

Good programs for the treatment of alcohol and drug dependence are available and the recovery rate is improving all the time. Most doctors, however, do not know where to go for help and are afraid to ask.

In treatment the doctor may encounter another problem—some find it difficult to accept the role of patient. It may be equally difficult for one doctor to treat another; all too often the relationship with a professional colleague prevents the physician-patient from getting the help he/she really needs.

The physician may be subject to financial pressure and feel that he or she cannot afford to be away from the practice, leaving the family with no income for several weeks. Putting off treatment won't help, however, and his/her financial affairs are likely to get worse until the physician gains control over the misuse of chemicals.

The Doctors on Chemicals (DOC) program continues to assist physicians who have become dependent on alcohol and/or drugs. The program is supported by the Education and Research Foundation of the College of Physicians and Surgeons of Ontario. Physicians may seek help directly by contacting the College or may be referred by a colleague or through the Ontario Medical Association.

The objective of the program is to ensure that a comprehensive service is available to members of the College in the form of counselling, treatment, rehabilitation, and follow-up while at the same time ensuring that the member is not a threat to self or to patients. So long as the affected member is receiving appropriate treatment and follow-up, the College usually has no need or interest in becoming formally involved. Many physicians who have recognized their dependence early have undergone treatment without it becoming known to the College that a problem existed. The College becomes involved in a formal manner only when the dependent physician fails to seek or to accept needed treatment and becomes a threat to patients. Physicians who prescribe for themselves are soon reported by the federal authorities to the College, which may then be forced to take formal action under the provisions of the Fitness to Practice Committee if the member does not agree to accept help voluntarily.

What Can You Do?

If it's not your problem, why should you do anything? Surely the physician on alcohol or drugs knows he or she is in trouble and may be jeopardizing both family life and professional career. If they know all this, why don't they stop? The simple answer is that without your help, they can't. Doctors who have gone through the experience will tell you they knew what they were doing to their families and to their own lives. They thought they could control their use of alcohol or drugs. They repeatedly and emphatically stated their desire and intention to do so. The fact that they were unable to maintain this control is no reflection on their characters—it is what dependence is all about. Don't miss an opportunity to help a colleague. Don't wait to be asked. Do what you can to persuade any doctor whom you believe to be dependent on drugs or alcohol to start treatment as soon as possible.

A member seeking advice and/or assistance may call the College and speak to a College officer or the College's Program Consultant, Dr. James Rankin. Dr. Rankin, who functions as an independent physician, is not on the College staff and is prohibited from reporting any information regarding examination or treatment of a member unless he receives the member's specific authorization to do so. Dr. Jack Saunders at the Ontario Medical Association may also be contacted for direction. All calls are confidential; the member is not obligated to identify him/herself. If the receiver of the call is unable to provide the assistance required, a doctor with knowledge and experience in the field will return the call as quickly as possible.

Dr. James Rankin   978-8634

Dr. Jack Saunders

963-9383

APPENDIX

This appendix lists the Addiction Research Foundation community services division offices and Ontario alcohol/drug assessment and referral centres and detoxification centres. For a comprehensive listing of services available throughout the province, Ontario physicians should consult the *Directory of Alcohol and Drug Treatment Resources in Ontario*, published by the Addiction Research Foundation.

Physicians outside the province should contact their local provincial or state alcohol and/or drug agencies for information on the resources available to them.

ADDICTION RESEARCH FOUNDATION
COMMUNITY SERVICES DIVISION OFFICES

For detailed information on treatment services offered please contact your local Addiction Research Foundation office.

BARRIE
100 Bell Farm Rd.
L4M 4Y5
(705) 726-4976

BELLEVILLE
248 Bridge St. East
K8N 1P1
(613) 962-9482

BURLINGTON
3425 Harvester Rd., Suite 211
L7N 3N1
(416) 632-2436, Ext. 38

CHATHAM
259 Wellington St. West
N7M 1J9
(519) 354-1000

CORNWALL
General Hospital
K6H 1Z5
(613) 932-3300, Ext. 238

HAMILTON
20 Hughson St. South, Suite 508
L8N 2A1
(416) 525-1250

KAPUSKASING
19B Riverside Dr.
P5N 1A4
(705) 335-6081

KENORA
115 Chipman St.
P9N 1V7
(807) 468-6372

KINGSTON
309 Alfred St.
K7L 3S4
(613) 546-4266

KITCHENER
639 King St. West
N2G 1C7
(519) 579-1310

LONDON
414 Dufferin Ave.
N6B 1Z6
(519) 433-3171

MISSISSAUGA
165 Dundas St. West, Suite 602
L5B 2N6
(416) 270-1431

NORTH BAY
288 Worthington St. West
P2B 3B4
(705) 472-3850

OSHAWA
44 Bond St. West, 10th Floor
L1G 1A4
(416) 576-6277

OTTAWA
880 Wellington St., Suite 800
K1R 6K7
(613) 238-8230, Ext. 1,2,5

OWEN SOUND
595 9th Ave. East (County Bldg.)
N4K 3E3
(519) 371-1861

PEMBROKE
98 Pembroke St.
K8A 5M6
(613) 735-1023

PERTH
39 Drummond St. West
K7H 2J9
(613) 267-1152

PETERBOROUGH
223 Aylmer St. North
K9J 3K3
(705) 748-9830

ST. CATHARINES
63 Church St., Suite 410
L2R 3C4
(416) 685-1361

SARNIA
265 North Front St., Suite 106E
(The Petrosar Bldg.)
N7T 5S6
(519) 337-9611

SAULT STE. MARIE
464 Albert St. East—Walrus II
P6A 2J8
(705) 256-2226

SIMCOE
191 Queensway West, Suite 1
N3Y 2M8
(519) 426-7260

SUDBURY
144 Pine St., Suite 203
P3C 1X3
(705) 675-1195

THUNDER BAY
West Arthur Place, Suite 104
1265 Arthur St. East
P7C 4X8
(807) 622-0607

TIMMINS
119 Pine St. South
Pine Plaza, 3rd Floor
P4N 2K3
(705) 267-6419

TORONTO
Addiction Research Foundation
33 Russell St.
M5S 2S1
(416) 595-6000

WINDSOR
2090 Wyandotte St. East
N8Y 1E6
(519) 253-1146

ONTARIO ALCOHOL/DRUG
ASSESSMENT AND REFERRAL CENTRES

BARRY'S BAY
St. Francis Alcohol Referral Centre
c/o St. Francis Memorial Hospital
K0J 1B0
(613) 756-3044

BELLEVILLE
Addiction Training and Assessment
  Counselling Inc. (ATAC)
218 Front St.
K8N 2Z2
(613) 962-5860

BRANTFORD
Alcohol and Drug Abuse Assessment
  and Referral Program
225 St. Paul Ave., 6th Floor
N3R 5Z3
(519) 753-7377, Ext. 22, 24, 25

BROCKVILLE
Addiction Assessment Centre
c/o Brockville General Hospital
75 Emma St.
K6V 1S8
(613) 345-5645, Ext. 163

BURLINGTON
Alcohol and Drug Addiction Program
  (ADAPT)
760 Brant St., Suite 407
L7R 4B7
(416) 639-6537

CHATHAM
Kent Alcohol Assessment, Referral,
  and Day-Care Program
c/o Chatham Public General Hospital
106 Emma St.
N7L 1A8
(519) 351-6144

GODERICH
Huron County Addiction
  Assessment and Referral Service
c/o Alexandra General Marine
  Hospital
120 Napier St.
N7A 1W5
(519) 524-7111

KAPUSKASING
North Cochrane Addiction Services
Service de Toxicomanie Inc.
  Cochrane Nord
19B Riverside Dr.
P5N 1A4
(705) 335-8408

KENORA
Kenora Alcohol and Drug
  Assessment Referral Centre
115 Chipman St.
P9N 1V7
(807) 468-6372

KINGSTON
Kingston Alcohol Referral Centre
  Inc.
131 Johnson St.
K7L 1X9
(613) 546-1758

KITCHENER
Waterloo Region Alcohol and
  Drug Assessment Service
637 King St. West
N2G 1C7
(519) 579-1870

LONDON
Assessment and Referral Centre
Box 338, Station "B"
N6A 4W1
(519) 439-4307

NAPANEE
Napanee Assessment/Referral Service
c/o Lennox and Addington County
    General Hospital
8 Park Dr.
K7R 2Z4
(613) 354-3301, Ext. 228

NEW LISKEARD
Tri-Town Alcohol and Drug
    Assessment Centre
c/o Temiskaming Health Unit
221 Whitewood Ave.
P0J 1P0
(705) 647-4306

NEWMARKET
Addiction Services for York Region
291 Davis Dr.
L3Y 2N6
(416) 898-5950

NORTH BAY
North Bay and Nipissing District
    Assessment/Referral and Primary
    Care Service
228 Worthington St. West
P1B 1G9
(705) 472-3850

OTTAWA
Addiction Assessment/Referral
    Service
880 Wellington St., Suite 800
K1R 6K7
(613) 238-8235

PEMBROKE
Renfrew County Alcohol and Drug
    Assessment/Referral Service
98 Pembroke St. West
K8A 5M6
(613) 735-1023

PERTH
Lanark, Leeds, Grenville
    Addiction Assessment and
    Referral Service
39 Drummond St. West
K7H 2J9
(613) 267-1152

PETERBOROUGH
Fourcast Assessment and Referral
    Service Inc.
295 Charlotte St.
K9J 2V6
(705) 876-1292

RENFREW
Renfrew Alcohol and Drug
    Assessment/Referral Service
c/o Renfrew Victoria Hospital
499 Raglan St. North
K7V 1P6
(613) 432-4851, Ext. 225

ST. CATHARINES
Niagara Alcohol and Drug
    Assessment Service
168 Ontario St., Unit 9
L2R 5K7
(416) 684-1183

SHARBOT LAKE
North Frontenac Community Services
Elizabeth St.
K0M 2P0
(613) 279-2928

STRATFORD
Perth Addiction Assessment Centre
380 Hibernia St.
N5A 5W3
(519) 271-6730

TORONTO
Clinical Institute
Addiction Research Foundation
33 Russell St.
M5S 2S1
(416) 595-6000

ONTARIO DETOXIFICATION CENTRES

HAMILTON
132 Wilson St. East
L8R 1E2
(416) 527-9264

KENORA
Alpha Delta Chi House
6 Matheson St. South
P9N 1T5
(807) 468-5631

KINGSTON
c/o Hotel Dieu Hospital
236-238 Brock St.
K7L 1S4
(613) 546-2771

KITCHENER
466 Park St.
N2G 1N6
(519) 749-4209

LONDON
St. Joseph's Detox
471 William St.
N6B 3E4
(519) 432-7241

OSHAWA
Pinewood Centre
300 Centre St.
L1H 4B2
(416) 723-8195

OTTAWA
Elizabeth Bruyere Detox
62 Bruyere St.
K1N 5M5
(613) 230-2108

ST. CATHARINES
10 Adams St.
L2R 2B8
(416) 682-7211

SAULT STE. MARIE
c/o Plummer Memorial Hospital
911 Queen St. East
P6A 2B6
(705) 942-1872

SUDBURY
69 Elm St. West
P3C 1T4
(705) 674-3330

THUNDER BAY
232 Camelot St.
P7A 4B2
(807) 344-7522

TORONTO

West Central Detox
16 Ossington Ave.
M6J 2Y7
(416) 533-7945

ARF Detox
410 Dundas St. West
M5T 1G7
(416) 977-4309

East General Detox
109 Knox Ave.
M4L 2P1
(416) 461-7408

St. Michael's Detox
314 Adelaide St. East
M5A 1N1
(416) 864-5078

St. Joseph's Detox
2769 Dundas St. West
M6P 1Y4
(416) 763-3533

WINDSOR
363 Mill St.
N9C 2R3
(519) 253-5503

INDEX

Acetaminophen
    overdose, 18
    toxic level of, 15,19
Acetylcysteine, 18-19
Addiction, 3
AIDS, 55
Alcohol
    blood levels of, 15
    carcinogenic effect of, 52
    coma, 15,20
    conversion diagram, 12
    dipstick, 16
    embryologic effect of, 52
    history re abuse, 8
    medical problems caused
      by, 46
    for methanol poisoning,
      20-21
    withdrawal seizures, 30-31
    withdrawal syndrome, 28-32
Alcoholic
    brain damage, 46
    cardiomyopathy, 51
    cirrhosis, 47
    gastritis, 47-48
    heart disease, 51
    hepatitis, 47
    hyperuricemia, 50
    hypoglycemia, 50
    ketoacidosis, 50
    liver disease, 47
    pancreatitis, 48
    thrombocytopenia, 49
Alcoholism
    and anemia, 49
    and cancer, 52
    cardiorespiratory
      complications of, 51
    definition of, 2
    and diabetes, 50
    diagnosis of, 6-10
    early identification of, 6

    endocrine
      complications of, 49-50
    epidemiology of, 3
    gastroenterological
      complications of, 47
    hematological complications
      of, 49
    history of, 8
    and hypertension, 51
    and infections, 52
    markers of, 7
    medical complications
      of, 46
    metabolic complications
      of, 50
    neurological complications
      of, 46
    and pregnancy, 52-53
Alkalinization of urine, 20,25
Amphetamines, 13,40
Amylase in pancreatitis, 48
Analgesic nephropathy, 55
Anemias, 49
Antabuse (see Disulfiram)
Antacids, 48
Anti-alcohol drugs, 58
Arrhythmias
    in alcoholic
      cardiomyopathy, 51
    in tricyclic overdose, 25
Aspirin (see Salicylate)
Ativan (see Lorazepam)

Bacterial endocarditis, 55
Bacterial peritonitis, 52
Barbiturates
    abuse of, 32
    intoxication, 20,33
    overdose, 20
    toxic levels of, 13
    withdrawal, 32-35

Benzodiazepines
    abuse, 35
    for alcohol
        withdrawal, 29-30
    equivalence table, 37
    withdrawal, 35-36
Blood alcohol level, 15
Blood drug levels, 15
Brain damage and alcohol, 46-47

C.A.G.E., 8
Calcium carbimide, 58-61
    contraindications, 61
    dose of, 59
    side effects of, 60
Cancer and alcohol, 52
Cannabis, 13,40
Cardiomyopathy (alcohol), 51
Cerebellar degeneration
    (alcohol), 47
Cerebral atrophy (alcohol), 46
Chronic pain and
    drug abuse, 42-43
Cimetidine, 48
Cirrhosis, 47
Clonidine
    for narcotic withdrawal, 39
Cocaine, 13,40
Coma (alcoholic), 15,20
Combination drugs, 41-42
Conversion diagram (alcohol), 12
Coronary artery disease, 51

Darvon (see Propoxyphene)
Delirium
    in alcohol withdrawal, 28
    in sedative-hypnotic
        withdrawal, 33
Delta, hepatitis, 54
Dependence
    physical, 2
    psychological, 2

Diabetes and alcoholism, 50
Diagnosis
    of alcoholism, 8-10
    of drug abuse, 13-15
Dialysis
    for methanol poisoning, 21
    for salicylate overdose, 25
Diazepam
    abuse of, 35
    for alcohol
        withdrawal, 29-30
    for benzodiazepine
        withdrawal, 36
    for psychedelic
        withdrawal, 40
    for withdrawal seizures, 30
Dilantin (see Phenytoin)
Dipstick (alcohol), 16
Disulfiram, 58-61
    contraindications, 61
    dose of, 59
    side effects of, 60
Doctors on chemicals, 62
Drug abuse
    and chronic pain, 42-43
    definition of, 2
    history, 14
    and infections, 53-55
    medical complications
        of, 53
    poly-drug, 41
Drug dependence, 2
Drug levels, 15

Early identification of alcohol
    problems, 6-8
Encephalopathy
    hepatic, 47
    glue sniffers', 56
Endocarditis of addicts, 55
Endocrine complications
    of alcoholism, 49-50

Enzyme abnormalities
(liver), 47,53
Epidemiology of alcoholism, 3
Epilepsy and alcohol, 31
Equivalents
benzodiazepines, 37
narcotics, 23
Esophagitis, 47
Ethanol (see Alcohol)

Family involvement, 61
Fatty liver, 47
Fetal alcohol syndrome, 52-53
Fiorinal, 41-42
Focal seizures, 31
Folate deficiency, 49

Gamma-GT and alcohol, 7
Gastritis, alcoholic, 47
Gastrointestinal complications of
alcoholism, 47
Glue sniffers' encephalopathy, 56

H₂ blockers, 48
Halcion (see Triazolam)
Haloperidol
for alcohol withdrawal, 30
for psychedelic
withdrawal, 20,40
Heart disease and alcohol, 51
Hematological complications of
alcoholism, 49
Hemodialysis (see Dialysis)
Hepatic encephalopathy, 47
Hepatitis
A, 53-54
alcoholic, 47
B, 53-54
delta, 54
immunoprophylaxis of, 54
investigation of, 53
viral, 53

Heroin (see Narcotics)
High-density lipoprotein and
alcohol, 7,51
Histories
re alcohol, 10
re psychoactive drugs, 14
Hypertension and alcohol, 51
Hypnotics (see Sedatives)
Hypoglycemia
alcoholic, 50

Infections, 52,53-55
Intoxications, 18-25
Ischemic heart disease, 51

Ketoacidosis, alcoholic, 50

Laboratory tests
(toxicology), 14-16
Liver disease
alcoholic, 47
viral, 53
Liver toxicity
acetaminophen, 18
Loading technique
with diazepam, 29
with phenobarbital, 34-35
Lorazepam
abuse, 36
for alcohol withdrawal, 30
LSD, 13,20,40

Macrocytosis
of alcoholism, 7,49
Mandrax (see Methaqualone)
Marijuana (see Cannabis)
Markers of alcoholism, 7
MCV and alcohol, 7,49

Medical complications
    of alcoholism, 46-53
    of drug abuse, 53-56
Metabolic complications
    of alcoholism, 50
Methadone
    for narcotic withdrawal, 39
Methanol (methylalcohol), 20-21
Methaqualone
    overdose, 21
    toxic level of, 15
Morphine (see Narcotics)

Naloxone
    challenge test, 38
    for narcotic overdose, 22
Narcotic
    overdose, 22-23
    relative potencies, 23
    withdrawal, 37-40
    withdrawal in pregnancy, 40
    withdrawal in surgery, 39
Nephropathy
    analgesic, 55
    heroin-induced, 55
Neurological complications
    (alcohol), 46-47
Neuropathy, 46
Novahistex, 42

Opiates (see Narcotics)
Organic brain syndrome
    (alcohol), 46
Overdoses
    acetaminophen, 18-20
    barbiturate, 20
    methaqualone, 21
    narcotic, 22
    salicylate, 24-25
    tricyclic
        antidepressants, 25

Oxazepam
    abuse, 36
    for alcohol withdrawal, 30

Pain and drug abuse, 42-43
Pancreatitis, 48-49
Paracentesis (diagnostic), 52
Parkinsonism and alcoholism, 47
PCP (see Phencyclidine)
Percocet, 42
Percodan, 41,42
Peritonitis, bacterial, 52
Phencyclidine, 13,23-24
Phenobarbital
    blood levels of, 15
    loading technique, 34-35
    for sedative-hypnotic
        withdrawal, 34
Phenytoin
    for alcohol
        withdrawal, 30-32
    for sedative-hypnotic
        withdrawal, 33
Physical dependence, 2
Physostigmine in tricyclic
        overdose, 26
Pneumonias in alcoholics, 52
Poisonings (see Overdoses)
Poly-drug abuse, 41
Pregnancy
    and alcoholism, 52-53
    and narcotics, 40
Prescription drug abuse, 42
Propoxyphene, 13,42
Propranolol
    for benzodiazepine
        withdrawal, 37
Protective drugs, 58
Pseudo-Cushing syndrome, 50
Pseudo-Parkinsonism, 47
Psychedelic drugs, 13,40
Psychoactive drug abuse, 14
Psychological dependence, 2

Psychoses
    drug induced, 40,56
Pulmonary edema in narcotic
    addicts, 55
Pulmonary talcosis, 55

Quaalude (see Methaqualone)

Ranitidine, 48
Rehabilitation from substance
    abuse, 58-65
Renal complications
    (narcotics), 55

Salicylate
    overdose of, 24-25
    toxic level of, 15,24-25
Sedatives (hypnotics)
    abuse of, 32
    intoxication, 20,33
    toxic levels of, 13
    withdrawal, 32-35
Seizures
    alcohol withdrawal, 30-31
    benzodiazepine
        withdrawal, 36
    focal, 31
    sedative-hypnotic
        withdrawal, 33
Serax (see Oxazepam)
Sexual dysfunction in
    alcoholism, 49-50
Sleep apnoea and alcohol, 51
Spontaneous peritonitis, 52
Status epilepticus, 31
Stimulant drugs, 13,40
Subdural hematoma, 47

Sucralfate, 48
Surgery and narcotics, 39

Temposil (see Calcium
    carbimide)
Thiamine, 28,29,46
Thrombocytopenia in
    alcoholism, 49
Tolerance, 3
Toxic drug levels, 15
Toxicology laboratory
    tests, 14-16
Trauma and alcohol, 7,9
Treatment of substance
    abuse, 58-65
Triazolam abuse, 36
Tricyclic overdose, 25
Tuinal, 42
Tussionex, 42
Tylenol, 42

Uric acid and alcohol, 7,50

Valium (see Diazepam)
Viral hepatitis, 53

Wernicke-Korsakoff
    syndrome, 46
Withdrawal
    alcohol, 28-32
    benzodiazepines, 35-36
    multiple drugs, 41
    narcotics, 37-40
    sedative-hypnotics, 32-35
    stimulant drugs, 40